THE MAKING OF A STRONG CULTURE
INTENTIONAL ORGANIZATIONS

Copyright © 2025 by Lepora Flournoy, PhD

ISBN: 979-8-9930919-2-1

All rights reserved. No part of this book may be reproduced, stored in a retrieval system, or transmitted in any form or by any means—electronic, mechanical, photocopying, recording, or otherwise—without the prior written permission of the publisher, except in the case of brief quotations embodied in critical articles or reviews.- per United States of America copyright law.

For Permissions, contact **info@nextgenpeople.com**

Printed in the United States of America

DEDICATION

This book is dedicated to the leaders of today—those navigating the fastest, most transformational, and most demanding times of our lifetime. It is for the leaders working relentlessly to make a difference, striving to elevate the people on their teams, strengthen their organizations, shape the marketplace, and impact the world.

TABLE OF CONTENTS

Preface I

Chapter 1: Introduction: How to Use This Book 11

Chapter 2: The Power of Culture—How Culture Connects It All and Shapes Us 18

Chapter 3: It's Not the One Right Culture, but the Strong Culture 24

Chapter 4: Intentionally Creating Culture: Building a Roadmap and Master Plan 52

Chapter 5: Igniting Organizational Heartbeat Engagement: Discretionary Effort, Loyalty, and Advocacy 87

Chapter 6: Case Studies: Lessons from Strong Cultures 98

Chapter 7: Transforming Culture 126

Chapter 8: The Impact of the Coronavirus Pandemic on Culture 148

Chapter 9: Generative AI and Its Impact on Culture: The New Presence in the Room 157

Chapter 10: The Death of Diversity in the US? 165

Chapter 11: Future State of Work and Impact on Culture 180

Chapter 12: Defining & Operationalizing Culture Strength 188

Chapter 13: Conclusion: You Choose—Intentionally Maintaining a Strong Culture or Playing Organizational Russian Roulette 203

Appendices 207

About the Author 254

PREFACE

I originally became interested in writing this book while working with a Fortune 500 company to help shift the organizational culture. As I sought resources, I realized that there were many well-written books about culture components used to engage employees. Other books addressed describing cultures that encouraged high-performing environments. However, I could not find a book that addressed the holistic creation and operationalization of organization culture or, as I like to call it, the organizational personality.

As I write this preface, I can't believe how long it has taken me to write this book. I have been writing it for three years now. While I resented the distractions and procrastinations, I am glad to have been able to include addressing monumental milestones currently and recently happening in our lifetime- AI, radical national culture transformation, diversity upheaval and global interactions like never seen before. I thank God that I kept the momentum all this time. Before diving into the deep end of this book once again, I researched to learn if someone else had tackled the journey that we are about to embark on. No, it still has not been done through the route that we are about to take.

There are many valuable books out there about organizational culture. Very good ones will be cited in this book as ideas are pulled to and from. However, what I have failed to find is a book that comprehensively and thoroughly tackles the process of creating and operationalizing an authentic organizational culture, an organization personality that transcends all industries and types of organizations. The focus of this book is on just that — painting the culture that you want to see. It is about demystifying what culture is. Not just about writing a pretty definition, but touching it, feeling it, pushing it, kicking it, pulling it back and at times blowing it up and starting all over again. We are talking about that physical tangibility of culture that defies the fluffy, feel-good, soft way that we have limited the definition of culture, in the past.

When we want stronger biceps, we do bicep curls. We may look in the mirror on a weekly basis and decide to add five pounds because we want our biceps to look bigger or stronger. Some will go on diets before a big beach trip. I've seen gym peers change their diets to lose five or 10 pounds. Each week, they adjust their calories in order to see the number on the scale that they want.

While we look at such efforts and agree that there is a causal relationship between the way that we eat, work out and how we look and make up our body composition. Very few will argue regarding the physical influential changes that can be seen.

I am here to tell you, remind you, that culture is just as manipulable as body weight, mass, muscle, the number on the scale. Culture, which I will also refer to as the organizational personality, is as easy to change, create, as 1, 2,3. Many people reading this right now will argue that that is bologna. You will recall the time that your organization attempted to change its culture or to get employees to do something that you wanted them to do. You will argue that employees left while you fought hard to create an engaging culture. Churches and civic organizations will argue that they attempt to create cultures of hospitality and yet have more in-fighting than you can afford. Sports teams are wondering how they can get everyone dedicated enough to win a game, or at least attend practices consistently.

Assuming that we were having such conversations live, I would say to you that one of two things are lacking, 1) honesty in what you truly want your culture to be and/or 2) willingness to pay for what you want your culture to be.

Regarding number one, organization leaders usually know the outcomes that they want to achieve, more revenue, more profits, faster productivity, loyal employees, fewer errors, customer retention, etc. When I think of organizations that have been successful in these areas over the past few decades- Google, Zappos, Apple, Chick-fil-A, GE, etc., they have one thing in common, for sure. They all have strong cultures. We will get into dissecting the various aspects that define culture. However, the term "strong" in this context is referring to the level of grasp that is held toward specific values and practices. Their cultures are very specific.

In their individual specificity, you will learn that each culture looks quite different from what you will find at any other organization. These organizations are courageously honest about what they truly want their organization personalities to be. They are not attempting to straddle the fence, please the world or bite their tongues regarding what is important to them.

The second mentioned reason why organizations fail to obtain the culture that they "want" is that they are not willing to pay for it. Where there are great rewards, great risks often precede. Every year, corporations, civic organizations, and teams develop their strategic plans for the future. They define where to place their efforts, money and risk. Prioritization is placed on goals and efforts based upon financial budget, level of risk aversion, values, financial and people goals.

While some organizations may be honest regarding what they want their culture or organization personality to be, they may not be willing to pay the price. That price might be in actual dollars, might be in time, power trade-offs, popularity decreases or other sacrificial investments. Ultimately, we know that there is a price to pay. The organizations that attain strong cultures are honest in what they want their culture to be and will double down on investing, paying the price over and over again, to attain and maintain that culture.

This book is about simplifying and operationalizing the process of making a culture, measuring that culture, tweaking and changing that culture along the way. This book is for those leaders who dare to take courageous accountability to make a culture.

What You Will Get Out of This Book

As you embark on this journey, you will find that this book serves as more than just a theoretical guide. It provides a comprehensive roadmap, enriched by historical context, case studies, and step-by-step instructions. Here's what you can expect to gain:

A Historical Perspective on Culture Creation:
Understanding how strong cultures have been built over time gives you a framework for what has worked, why it worked, and how to avoid common pitfalls.

A Roadmap for Building Culture:
Practical insights and processes that you can implement to build and nurture your own organizational culture.

Lessons from Real-World Examples:
Case studies from a variety of organizations-ranging from corporations to nonprofits to military units-that illustrate the principles of strong culture in action.

Key Traits and Behaviors:
Insight into the building blocks of strong cultures, including traits such as courage, honesty, and consistency, and how to promote shared identity among team members.

Strategies for Engagement and Loyalty:
Methods for fostering an environment where team members go above and beyond, cultivate loyalty, and become promoters of your culture.

Practical Tools and Techniques:
Tips for measuring culture and aligning your organization's structure and strategy to support the culture you intend to build.

Guidance for Cultural Transformation:
Learn when and how to change your culture when necessary, supported by frameworks such as the ADKAR model.

Operationalization of Culture:
Understand how to define and operationalize your culture by embedding practices, structures, and rituals that make it a natural part of your organization's daily operations.

Measuring and Sustaining Culture:
Learn to measure the relationship between your culture and desired business outcomes through effective tools and assessment techniques, and how to sustain it over time to keep it vibrant and adaptive.

A Forward-Looking Perspective:
Insights into the future of work, including trends in the gig economy, hybrid work, and globalization that impact culture-building.

CHAPTER 1

INTRODUCTION
HOW TO USE THIS BOOK

You may have heard the phrase by Peter Drucker that, "Culture eats strategy for breakfast." While I definitely agree that culture has the longest impact on any business outcome, I would say that culture should not be in competition with strategy at an organization, but culture should be a strategy of your organization. Culture should be an intentional strategy that supports who the organization wants to be and where the organization wants to go.

This book is your comprehensive guide to understanding, creating, and operationalizing organizational culture—what I like to call the "organizational personality." This book will guide you through the entire process of making culture tangible, measurable, and adaptable.

Culture is often perceived as an abstract concept, shrouded in ambiguous language and intangible ideas. The purpose of this book is to break down those perceptions, demystify the idea of culture, and turn it into a clear, actionable framework that leaders and organizations can use to transform their environments. Whether you are a business executive, a team leader, or an organizational consultant, this book will serve as your road map.

The hope is that you will use this book to
1. Understand the true definition of culture
2. Appreciate culture as a tangible, measurable asset, not a fluffy, amorphous mystery.
3. Be motivated to reap the benefits for your organization tied to intentionally creating and monitoring the culture of your organization.
4. Know how to operationalize, measure toward, and sustain the desired culture.
5. Identify, assess and adjust the impact of your organization's intentional culture on desired business outcomes.

Culture is your organization's personality and what your employees and team members use to guide their behavior. Before we go any further, let's align on some meanings as we discuss how to use this book.

1. **Culture:** When culture is referenced in the book, the assumed definition is "the set of shared values, beliefs, norms, and practices that shape the behavior and decision-making processes within an organization" as defined in the Cambridge Dictionary.

Every organization, large or small, has a culture. There are many types of organizations there, large and small corporations, working teams, churches, nonprofit organizations, sports teams, social organizations, nations, provinces, states, extended families, and nuclear families. Where we have more than one person who gathers with a cadence of regularity, we will find a culture. The culture is the manifested contract of the organization. It is more important than the contract itself because it reflects what actually happens. Oftentimes, we have organizational contracts that we agree upon verbally or nonverbally, yet the level that we adhere to that contract varies. This brings us to the next, very important term, with which we should align: Strong Culture.

2. **Strong Culture:** In this book, strong culture is defined as a culture that is very specific in defining their shared values, beliefs, norms and practices of their organization AND behave with strong adherence to their stated shared values, beliefs, norms and stated practices.

The strength of the culture is not defined in a normative manner, giving or taking away assigned value to the health or success of the organization. The strength of the culture is agnostic to any specific description of the organization beyond the level of intention and adherence to the chosen values by the organization. Regarding the health of a culture, let's align regarding how we define a healthy culture.

3. **Healthy Culture:** A healthy culture is a culture that drives the organization's desired outcomes.

If you Google or read about healthy cultures, you will find a plethora of organizational descriptions. However, to use culture as a tool, you have to first decide what you desire to accomplish. In addition, you have to take into consideration the context, including challenges, obstacles, support and level of such factors. The purpose of this book and culture model is use culture as an active tool to achieve your organization's goals. For example, if you garden with soft earth, you may attempt to manually till the ground with a large fork or hoe. However, if you live somewhere where the ground is very difficult, and the earth is drier and harder to break, then you might go for a cultivator or a mechanical tiller. Culture can be used similarly in the sense that the elements that make up your culture should support your goal in the context in which you operate. That context is made up of your country, industry, competition, resources, etc. Every factor that can influence your organization makes up the context of your culture.

4. **Organization goals** are the goals that your entire organization agrees that you are working toward. The goals are linked to the vision and mission of your organization. If you are a corporation, such goals may be tied to revenue, cost savings, production accuracy, etc. Churches may have such goals including number of people baptized, number of members, number of people served. Civic and policy organizations may have goals tied to lowering negative incident rates. For example, MADD, Mothers Against Drunk Driving, has studied the correlation between its advertisements and incidents of drunk driving. Whatever the vision, mission and organization goals of your organization, by the culture that you choose, influence, and practice. Other organizational goals include reduction of carbon footprint, community service hours, Net Promoter Score (NPS), etc.

There are literally hundreds of types of organizational goals. What is equally important to identifying such goals is prioritizing these goals. These goals drive the time and energy effort of your entire organization, or at least they should. The commitment to your organization's culture should be directly related to your organizational goals.

Welcome to The Making of a Culture: A Roadmap to Building Intentional Organizations. Whether you are a CEO, seasoned leader, an entrepreneur, executive director, pastor, a manager, and family leader or someone fascinated by the dynamics of how organizations create and sustain cultures, this book is designed with you in mind. The topic of culture in organizations has been discussed extensively, often veiled in abstraction and theory, but this book seeks to offer something different: a practical, history-backed roadmap that demystifies culture-building and provides actionable steps for creating strong, intentional cultures within any type of organization.

What This Book is Not

It's important to understand what this book is not so that you can set appropriate expectations. The Making of a Culture is not:

- **A Quick Fix:** Building a strong, intentional culture takes time. This book will provide you with tools and knowledge, but it will not instantly transform your organization overnight.
- **A One-Size-Fits-All Guide:** Every organization is unique, and while the principles here are adaptable, they need to be tailored to your specific context and objectives.
- **A Judgment on the "Right" Culture:** This book does not prescribe a "best" culture; it guides you in creating a culture that suits your organization's purpose and needs. The focus is on creating a strong culture that aligns with desired behaviors, not passing judgment on whether those behaviors are morally or ethically superior.

What You Can Accomplish

If you engage with this book thoughtfully and apply its principles, you can accomplish the following:

- **Create a Blueprint for Culture:** Develop a detailed, actionable plan that outlines how to build or strengthen your organization's culture.
- **Establish Consistent Behaviors:** Implement structures and systems that encourage and reward behaviors aligned with your organization's goals.
- **Boost Engagement and Retention:** Foster an environment where people feel connected, valued, and motivated to contribute their best efforts.
- **Operationalize Your Culture:** Gain the ability to embed cultural practices seamlessly into the daily operations and processes of your organization.
- **Measure Cultural Impact:** Learn how to measure and assess the relationship between your culture and the desired business outcomes, ensuring that your efforts align with strategic objectives.
- **Sustain Culture Over Time:** Build a resilient culture that can be maintained, adapted, and refreshed as your organization evolves and faces new challenges.
- **Adapt to Change:** Equip yourself with the tools needed to recognize when cultural shifts are necessary and how to implement them effectively.
- **Leave with a Renewed Appreciation for Culture's Role:** Gain a deeper understanding of the power of culture and how it underpins every aspect of an organization's success.

How to Use This Book to maximize the value of this book:

- **Read Actively:** Take notes, highlight key points, and think about how each concept applies to your current or future organization.
- **Reflect on Case Studies:** Analyze the case studies provided and compare them to your organization. What can you learn, emulate, or avoid?
- **Engage in Exercises:** This book can be used for Teams. It can be used as a workshop tool for HR leaders and consultants. Throughout the book, you'll find activities, exercises, and reflection prompts. Use these sections as starting points for group discussions, workshops, or training sessions. Use them for team engagement and/or to solidify your understanding and start applying these lessons as a leader yourself.
- **Discuss with Peers:** Culture is a collective effort. Share your insights and discuss key points with your team or other leaders to build consensus and momentum.

How to Use this Book

To Maximize the Value of this book

Read Actively

Take notes, highlight key points, and think about how each concept applies to your current or future organization.

Reflect on Case Studies

Analyze the case studies provided and compare them to your organization. What can you learn, emulate, or avoid?

Engage in Exercises

This book can be used for Teams, It can be used as a workshop tool for HR leaders and consultants. Throughout the book, you'll find activities, exercises and reflection prompts. Use these sections as starting points for group discussions, workshops, or training sessions, workshops, or training sessions. Use them for team engagement and/or to solidify your understanding and start applying these lessons as a leader yourself.

Discuss with Peers

Culture is a collective effort. Share your insights and discuss key points with your team or other leaders to build consensus and momentum.

This book is more than a passive read; it's an invitation to become an architect of culture within your organization. With an open mind and a willingness to apply these concepts, you'll be on your way to fostering a strong, purposeful, and resilient culture.

Culture is a force multiplier. A well-defined and operationalized culture leads to higher productivity, employee engagement, retention, and profitability. Leaders who are serious about creating a sustainable competitive advantage will find that culture.

CHAPTER 2
THE POWER OF CULTURE—HOW CULTURE CONNECTS IT ALL AND SHAPES US

Introduction to Culture's Role and Significance

A CEO once sat across from me at a long oak table, arms folded, eyes skeptical.

"Culture is soft stuff," he said. "We need to focus on the real drivers of performance."

I smiled. "Exactly. Culture is the real driver," I replied, sliding over turnover reports and engagement data. Six months later, his organization's productivity was up, attrition was down, and that same CEO was talking about culture in every town hall.

Culture is not soft. It is not optional. It is not decorative. Culture is the operating system of your organization. It shapes how people think, behave, relate, and perform. Whether intentionally crafted or passively inherited, every organization has one. The question is not if culture exists, but whether yours is helping or hurting you.

From the largest nations to the smallest families, culture defines the rules of the game. It determines how power is exercised, how decisions are made, how success is defined, and how people show up. In organizations, culture is the invisible force that connects vision to execution, people to purpose, and intention to behavior.

Culture also holds memory. It carries pride, pain, and promise. It shows how things have always been done while quietly pointing to what people long for next. Culture is both mirror and map—reflecting reality and guiding future possibility. If you know how to read it, you can transform it. If you ignore it, it will quietly control your outcomes.

Defining Culture and Its Core Components

Culture is more than a vibe or mission statement. It is the sum of assumptions, values, behaviors, rituals, symbols, and systems that guide how things get done. Anthropologists call it a shared way of life. Leaders should call it their most powerful tool.

It has both visible and invisible layers. The visible includes dress codes, office design, logos, and recognition programs. The invisible—tone, unwritten rules, and which behaviors are rewarded or ignored—are harder to see but infinitely more powerful.

Think of culture like an iceberg. Above the waterline are the slogans and policies. Below it are the assumptions, power dynamics, and hidden rules that actually drive decisions. Real change always begins below the surface.

Culture is fluid. It is shaped by history, leadership, environment, and the behavior of the most powerful people in the room. It can shift slowly over decades or overnight in a crisis. But it is never neutral—it is always enabling or resisting.

The Influence of Organizational Culture on Identity

Walk into a new organization, and you feel it instantly. Before you memorize the mission statement, you start adapting. You shift your tone. You adjust your habits. You watch how people interact and take mental notes. You are being shaped.

Culture forms identity—not just collective identity, but individual identity. When people say, "This place changed me," they mean the culture reshaped how they see themselves.

Sometimes that shift is empowering. People become more confident, more collaborative, more curious. Other times, it is stifling. They shrink, conform, or burn out. The message of the culture is: "To belong here, you must be like this."

I once coached a brilliant woman muted by the culture of a large nonprofit. Her ideas were innovative, but the culture rewarded tradition and conformity. Over time, she began doubting herself. Once she realized the issue wasn't her capacity but the culture she was embedded in, she found the courage to speak up and eventually led a transformation effort.

The culture had been a container that compressed her. With intention, she turned it into one that could amplify her. That is the power of culture: it does not just drive performance metrics; it shapes human lives.

Culture as a Unifying Force

When culture is aligned, it acts like a superconductor. It reduces friction, builds trust, and creates shared meaning. Culture turns a collection of people into a community. You see it in military units, startups, faith communities, and sports teams. There's a rhythm, shorthand, and set of references that make the group move as one.

Rituals often carry this unifying power: the weekly stand-up, the onboarding buddy system, the open-door policy that leaders actually use. These are not cosmetic. They are culture in motion.

Unity, however, does not require uniformity. The strongest cultures create cohesion not by enforcing sameness, but by elevating shared purpose. When the "why" is clear, people can bring their own "how."

Great cultures don't ask people to hide who they are. They make people feel like they belong because of who they are.

The Dual Nature of Culture

Culture unites, but it also divides. It always creates insiders and outsiders.

In one client engagement, the dominant culture celebrated extroversion, constant availability, and informal networking. This wasn't in the handbook, but it was everywhere in practice. As a result, thoughtful and strategic employees—many from different cultural or neurodiverse backgrounds—felt invisible. Not because they lacked capability, but because the culture didn't know how to see them.

When culture is too narrow, it becomes brittle. Innovation stalls. Talent leaves. Inclusion falters. A culture becomes a gatekeeper rather than a catalyst.

Strong cultures are not just defined by what they value, but by how they handle what they don't understand. Do they silence dissent or learn from it? Do they resist new voices or integrate them? A truly inclusive culture doesn't avoid conflict. It learns to navigate it, mine it, and grow from it.

Culture either aligns these elements or makes them clash. Alignment creates trust. Misalignment creates exhaustion.

Culture and Global Challenges

In today's world of climate crisis, inequity, political instability, and disruption, culture is not just a competitive advantage—it is a survival imperative.

The COVID-19 pandemic revealed this vividly. Cultures built on trust and flexibility adapted quickly. Fear-based cultures clung to old habits and fractured. Remote work wasn't just a logistical shift—it was a cultural reckoning.

Culture also shapes how organizations handle social responsibility. Some embed sustainability into promotion criteria, vendor selection, and celebrations. Others treat it as a PR campaign. The difference is whether sustainability is cultural or performative.

As organizations become more diverse and globally spread, leaders need cultural agility: the ability to respect and adapt across contexts. This is no longer optional. It is the baseline for global leadership.

Culture's Influence on Strategy, Structure, Systems, and People

The McKinsey 7S model reminds us that organizations are webs of interconnected parts: Strategy, Structure, Systems, Skills, Style, Staff, and Shared Values. Culture runs through them all.

Strategy
A bold, risk-taking strategy will fail in a culture that punishes mistakes. A collaborative strategy will struggle in a culture that rewards lone heroes.

Structure
A flat org chart won't function in a hierarchical culture. People will still defer to power brokers. Culture defines how authority really flows.

Systems
Systems codify culture. If you say collaboration matters but reward only individual performance, your systems contradict your words.

Skills
Culture signals what's worth learning. A culture that avoids feedback will never grow coaching skills. A culture that values relationship will invest in emotional intelligence.

Style
Leadership style sets the emotional tone. Authority, service, consensus, or charisma, each reinforces or reshapes culture.

Staff
Who gets hired and promoted speaks louder than any values statement. Talent decisions are cultural declarations.

Shared Values
These are the glue, but only if they live in decisions, budgets, and consequences, not just posters.

Conclusion: Embracing Cultural Complexity

Culture is not wallpaper. It is architecture. It shapes how people move, what they believe is possible, and how they connect. And every culture tells a story—about what matters, who belongs, and how we grow.

If you want to change results, you have to change culture. Not with slogans, but with practice. Not by fixing people, but by reshaping the environment they work in.

The leaders who will shape the future are those who can read culture like a map, lead it like a story, and build it like a cathedral. Not for optics, but for impact.

Because in the end, culture is not just about how we work. It's about who we become while we're working.

CHAPTER 3

IT'S NOT THE ONE RIGHT CULTURE, BUT THE STRONG CULTURE

Introduction: What Is Strong Culture?

I remember sitting with the COO of a fast-scaling tech nonprofit that had just made a splash in the media for its rapid growth and innovative model. They were hiring fast, expanding globally, and attracting millions in funding. And yet, she leaned across the table and whispered, "We're winning everywhere, except inside."

This is the quiet confession behind many so-called success stories. Outward metrics look great, but inside? Decision-making is foggy, departments are misaligned, and leadership is exhausted from putting out fires. What's missing isn't capability; it's culture. More specifically, **strong culture.**

Let's be clear from the start: **Strong doesn't mean good.** Just like muscles can be used to hug or to harm, cultural strength is about consistency and intensity, not virtue. There are strong cultures that are toxic, and weak cultures with the kindest people you'll ever meet.

What makes a culture "strong" is its ability to clearly shape behavior across the organization. Strong cultures produce predictable reactions, shared assumptions, and internal clarity, even if the external world is in chaos.

Beyond the Surface: Schein's 3 Levels of Culture

To understand culture deeply, Edgar Schein gives us a framework that still holds power today. He describes three levels:

1. Artifacts, what we can see: the logos, office layout, dress code, website tone, perks. These are visible but don't explain much.
2. Espoused Values, what organizations say they believe: mission statements, guiding principles, DEI promises, leadership slogans.
3. Underlying Assumptions, the unconscious norms and default behaviors that actually drive decisions and actions. This is where real culture lives.

A strong culture exists when these three levels align. When what you see matches what's said, and what's said matches what's done. A weak culture shows up in the gaps, when the slide deck says "collaboration," but the bonus system rewards lone wolves.

Subcultures and Microcultures

Culture is not one monolith. In fact, every organization is a culture made of cultures. Engineering may have a different rhythm than HR. Regional offices may interpret values differently. Inside departments, you'll often find "microcultures" formed around influential leaders or legacy norms.

Strong culture doesn't mean identical culture throughout. It means that even when things are localized, there is a core cultural code that remains recognizable. It's like hearing a jazz trio take liberties with the melody but always returning to the same refrain. Strong cultures allow variation, but never confusion.

Culture in Action: BMW, Google, and Amazon

Look at BMW. Their obsession with precision and quality is not just a brand, it's a lived cultural experience. Every designer, engineer, and plant manager breathes the air of "premium." That's a strong culture.

Google, on the other hand, built its culture around curiosity and autonomy. From open workspaces to 20 percent innovation time, they infused experimentation into how they worked long before it was fashionable.

And then there's Amazon. Love them or not, they've created a culture of customer obsession and operational intensity. Jeff Bezos didn't just make it a motto; he built it into their hiring, leadership principles, and daily meetings. Everyone knows what the North Star is, and that clarity fuels speed.

None of these cultures are the same. But they are all strong because they are coherent, reinforced, and internalized.

The Core Idea: Consistency Over Content

Here's what it all comes down to: It's not about having the "right" culture. It's about having a culture that is real, consistent, and strong enough to shape behavior.

You don't need to copy Google or chase the newest trend on LinkedIn. Your organization's culture should reflect your purpose, your people, and your priorities. A strong culture is not built by imitation, but by integration, aligning what you believe with how you operate.

When culture is strong, people don't need a rulebook for every situation. They instinctively know what to do, how to decide, and how to show up. That's what frees organizations to move fast, build trust, and hold their center in times of change.

And in today's world of uncertainty, disruption, and reinvention, culture isn't just your soft side. It's your survival strategy.

Defining Strong Culture: Traits, Benefits, and Misconceptions

I was working with a faith-based organization that had recently undergone a leadership change. The new executive director had big ideas and an inspiring vision, but within six months, the staff was disengaged, turnover was climbing, and the energy that had once been palpable was gone. What went wrong? They had changed leadership, updated the website, and even launched a flashy new internal campaign about "transformation." But they never actually changed the culture. They tried to swap optics for alignment.

Let's say this clearly: Strong culture is not about perks. It is not about polished slogans or trendy tools. It is not a mimicry of what worked for another organization. Strong culture is about clarity. It is about behavior. It is about trust that builds through consistency over time.

Too many organizations make culture a branding exercise. They chase the language of innovation without committing to the discomfort that real innovation requires. Or they copy a competitor's talent strategy without realizing it was built for a totally different DNA. Culture, when done right, is not a cosmetic change. It is a full-body transformation.

The Real Markers of Strength

So what are we really talking about when we talk about strong culture?

- People at every level know what behaviors are expected and which are rewarded.
- There is alignment between what leaders say and what they do.
- The Value of the organization show up in how meetings are run, how performance is evaluated, and how mistakes are handled.
- Decision-making patterns are consistent and clear.

In strong cultures, people are not constantly guessing. They don't live in ambiguity. They are not afraid to act because they know what the organization wants. They trust that the unwritten rules won't contradict the written ones. That kind of clarity unleashes energy.

Weak cultures, on the other hand, live in the land of mixed signals. You hear one thing from the stage, another in your department, and something completely different when you watch who gets promoted. It creates cultural whiplash, and people respond by playing it safe, shutting down, or quietly leaving.

The Dangers of Uncertainty

Uncertainty is the breeding ground for disengagement. When people aren't sure how decisions are made, they stop bringing new ideas. When they don't know what leadership values, they spend more time navigating politics than doing meaningful work. When values feel vague or performative, people question whether their efforts even matter.

In uncertain cultures, middle managers become translators, trying to bridge the gap between conflicting signals. Teams spend emotional energy interpreting behaviors rather than producing results. And leaders burn out trying to fix what culture never clarified.

Contrast that with a strong culture, where even during crisis or change, people stay grounded. They know what the organization stands for. They know how to move. That kind of cultural strength becomes a source of resilience.

Key Outcomes of Weak vs. Strong Cultures

Let's look at what this actually creates over time:

Weak Culture Produces:

Fear-based decision-making, where leaders over-rely on control and micromanagement rather than empowering teams. **01**

High turnover and disengagement, as people leave for organizations where they feel seen, safe and valued. **02**

Siloed teams and internal turf wars, with departments hoarding information instead of sharing resources. **03**

Slow innovation and risk avoidance, as people fear failure more than they seek opportunity **04**

05

Cynicism and internal gossip, which erodes trust and drains momentum.

Strong Culture Produces:

06 Faster alignment and decision-making, because everone operates from the same shared principles.

07 Higher retention and better recruiting, since people want to stay where feel purposeful and seen.

08 Turst-based collaboration, where teams can challenge each other without fear, and accountability is matual.

09 More innovation and learning from failure, because the environment supports experimentation and safetly.

10 Deepened sense of belonging and shared purpose, where peole find meaning beyond their job description.

According to Deshpande et al. (1993), and I agree, strong cultures need clear answers to key questions:

1. What principles will we never compromise on?
2. What do we believe will always be right?
3. What limits will we accept to achieve success?
4. What is the minimum behavior we will accept?
5. How important are our employees or members?
6. How important are our customers?
7. How important is profit?
8. How do we treat organization property and resources?

These aren't rhetorical questions. They are the non-negotiables that shape what your culture feels like in everyday decisions. If your answers are vague or inconsistent, your culture will be too.

Strong cultures do not require perfection. They require consistency. They require leaders to name what matters, model it relentlessly, and design systems that reinforce it.

There is no "one" strong culture. But every strong culture shares one trait: It shapes how people behave without having to control them. That is the foundation we build from next.

Core Traits of Strong Cultures

When you examine strong cultures across sectors, you begin to see a shared DNA. These organizations, whether corporate, civic, nonprofit, or faith-based, all exhibit a few core traits that make their cultures feel alive, authentic, and deeply rooted.

Intentionality: Deliberate Choices and Alignment

Strong cultures are built, not inherited. They emerge when leadership makes deliberate choices about what to value, how to behave, and what to reward. This intentionality shows up in hiring, in strategic planning, in meeting rhythms, and in how people are promoted. Nothing is accidental. Alignment is not something hoped for, it is engineered.

Intentional cultures ask the hard questions and make the uncomfortable calls. If collaboration is a value, then compensation structures are built to reflect that. If diversity is a priority, then systems are audited for bias and inequity. Intentionality moves values off the wall and into the way people live and work.

Authenticity: No Polishing, No Pretending

People can smell performative culture from across the hallway. Authentic cultures don't pretend to be perfect. They don't sell one version of the organization in onboarding and deliver another in daily life. They are honest about who they are, what they value, and where they are still growing.

Authenticity breeds trust. When leaders admit mistakes, when culture is lived at the top and the bottom, and when people are allowed to show up as themselves, the organization becomes a space where real work and real change can happen. It is not about being polished. It is about being honest.

Operationalized Values: Embedded Into Decisions, Systems, and Interactions

A value that cannot be traced in daily behavior is not a value. It is a decoration. Strong cultures don't just name their values, they build systems, habits, and language around them. You see it in how meetings are run, how feedback is given, how conflict is handled, and how decisions are made.

Operationalized values mean that culture is not an HR initiative, it is an organizational backbone. It shows up in hiring scorecards, in strategic priorities, in performance reviews, and even in how a crisis is managed. When values are operationalized, they do not require reminders. They guide behavior automatically.

These three traits—intentionality, authenticity, and operationalized values—are not just abstract ideals. They are the roots from which cultural strength grows. And if we want to transform culture, we start by asking how deeply these roots have taken hold.

Benefits of a Strong Culture

Strong culture is not a background feature. It is the operating system beneath every decision, interaction, and result. It does not just keep things moving smoothly, it accelerates clarity, builds trust faster, and acts as a force multiplier across the organization. While strategies may shift and structures may evolve, culture remains the spine that holds everything together. And when it is strong, that spine does more than support. It leads.

Faster Decision-Making

When culture is strong, people do not need a playbook for every decision. They know the guardrails. They know what the organization would choose, even when leadership is not in the room. This cultural clarity becomes a filter that allows decisions to move faster and with more confidence. Meetings are shorter, approvals are quicker, and more time is spent building rather than just aligning.

Behavioral Alignment

In a strong culture, values and behaviors match. This alignment means fewer surprises, fewer performance issues, and more consistent execution. You don't need to micromanage when the culture is clear. Expectations are baked in. Behavior is not driven by the mood of the week, but by deep-rooted understanding of what the organization stands for and how it operates.

Attraction and Retention

People stay where they feel clear, challenged, and connected. Strong cultures attract talent not just through compensation, but through identity. People want to belong to something that is bold, consistent, and meaningful. And once they are inside, they tend to stay longer and refer others who fit. Recruitment becomes a magnet, not a struggle.

Resilience Under Pressure

When a crisis hits, weak cultures scramble. Strong cultures hold. Cultural clarity allows teams to adapt without losing direction. Values serve as a compass. Even when structures or strategies shift, the core remains. This resilience is what helps organizations emerge from hardship stronger, not just scarred.

Deeper Meaning and Engagement

Strong culture turns a job into a calling. People understand not just what they are doing, but why it matters. They find connection in a shared purpose. Engagement is not measured only by productivity but by emotional commitment. People go the extra mile not out of fear, but because they care. That kind of discretionary effort is not bought, it is cultivated.

The benefits of a strong culture compound over time. They create speed, trust, and meaning—the three things every leader wishes they had more of. And the good news is, they are not accidental. They are built.

Defining Strong Culture: Traits, Benefits, and Misconceptions

I was working with a faith-based organization that had recently undergone a leadership change. The new executive director had big ideas and an inspiring vision, but within six months, the staff was disengaged, turnover was climbing, and the energy that had once been palpable was gone. What went wrong? They had changed leadership, updated the website, even launched a flashy new internal campaign about "transformation." But they never actually changed the culture. They tried to swap optics for alignment.

Let's say this clearly: Strong culture is not about perks. It is not about polished slogans or trendy tools. It is not a mimicry of what worked for another organization. Strong culture is about clarity. It is about behavior. It is about trust that builds from consistency over time.

Too many organizations make culture a brand exercise. They chase the language of innovation without committing to the discomfort that real innovation requires. Or they copy a competitor's talent strategy without realizing it was built for a totally different DNA. Culture, when done right, is not a cosmetic change. It is a full-body transformation.

Here are some new behavioral indicators that distinguish strong cultures:

Time Orientation

People know whether the organization is guided by legacy, present priorities, or long-term possibilities—and behaviors reflect that consistently.

Use of Physical Space

Workspaces reinforce collaboration, focus, or hierarchy based on strategic cultural intention—not trend or chance.

Spending Philosophy

Budgets mirror priorities. If people are your value, they see it in the investment. If innovation matters, it's resourced.

Decision-Making Style

Teams know when decisions are top-down, collaborative, or delegated—and act without second-guessing the norms.

Individual Accountability vs. Collective Ownership

Whether driven by singular leadership or team-based consensus, the decision logic is transparent and accepted.

Risk Tolerance

People take bold action or cautious steps with confidence because they know what the culture rewards and protects.

Innovation Orientation

New ideas are celebrated or carefully tested, depending on how the organization frames its learning environment.

Learning and Development

Growth is prioritized visibly through coaching, formal programs, or hands-on exposure, as matched to cultural commitments.

Communicaation Style

Whether blunt or diplomatic, communication is not a guessing game - teams learn to trust the tone.

Customer Orientation

Employees operate with shared clarity on how central the customer is in daily work and long-term success.

Employee Orientation

There's no ambiguity on how employees are valued - from compensation to wellness to voice.

Profit Orientation

There's no hidden message about what matters more: mission, margin, or both.

Conformity vs. Inclusion

The level of flexibility or expected assimilation is known. People feel safe to adapt or align.

Work-Life Harmony

Employees know whether the culture prizes intensity or sustainability - and decisions mirror that.

Ethics and Integrity

Integrity is not aspirational, it is practiced. People know what lines cannot be crossed.

Internal Focus vs. Community Responsibility

Culture makes it clear whether change starts inside or include serving outsides stakeholders.

Quality Operations Standards

Teams know the level of quality expected. Exellence is defined and embedded.

When these indicators are aligned, organizations don't need to control behavior. People instinctively operate from the culture, because they trust it. That is the true measure of cultural strength.

Relationships: The Social Fabric of Strong Culture

In every strong culture I've studied or worked with, one thing always stands out: people don't just work together, they belong together. Relationships are not side effects of a good culture. They are the scaffolding that holds it up.

A strong culture doesn't just define what people do. It defines how they treat one another. Whether in a corporate boardroom, a nonprofit program team, or a civic planning committee, the emotional tone of relationships reveals the true health of the culture. In a weak culture, relationships are transactional and cautious. People protect themselves first. In a strong culture, relationships are rooted in mutual respect, trust, and shared accountability. People don't just protect their turf, they protect the team.

You can't scale culture without relational trust. You can roll out new strategy decks, value statements, or even incentive plans, but none of that sticks if people do not trust the people they work with. And trust is not built from one team-building event. It is built from small, consistent behaviors: showing up on time, following through, giving feedback directly and kindly, sharing credit, admitting faults.

Strong cultures normalize these relational behaviors. They embed them in how feedback is given, how meetings are run, and how conflict is addressed. They build rituals that bind people together, storytelling at the start of team meetings, peer recognition moments, or quiet time before critical discussions. These rituals are not fluff. They are the emotional rhythm of the organization.

Strong culture also protects relationships when tension arises. It doesn't avoid conflict; it gives it a pathway. Feedback is expected, not feared. Disagreements are framed as learning moments, not political grenades. In that kind of environment, people can take risks together because they know the relational equity exists to recover.

Relational health is also where inclusion lives or dies. If people don't feel seen, heard, and respected by their colleagues, no DEI policy will make them feel safe. Inclusion is relational before it is structural. It is emotional before it is procedural.

One of the most overlooked truths in culture work is this: the speed of trust determines the speed of execution. When teams trust each other, they don't spend time second-guessing, triangulating, or polishing every sentence. They move. They stretch. They challenge each other with compassion. And they deliver results faster, not by force but by flow.

Relationships, then, are not a soft side of culture. They are the infrastructure of trust that makes strong culture possible. Without them, even the best strategy will fall flat.

Leadership: Culture's Loudest Messenger

A leader once told me, "I don't have time to be the culture champion." I told her, "Then you're already shaping the culture, just not intentionally." Leadership is never neutral. Whether active or passive, bold or hesitant, every leader broadcasts the culture. The only question is, are they reinforcing what you say you value, or quietly eroding it?

In strong cultures, leadership is not just a title, it is a signal. What leaders tolerate becomes permission. What they reward becomes aspirational. What they model becomes the unwritten rule. If a leader preaches collaboration but promotes lone heroes, the culture will tilt toward individualism regardless of the vision statement.

Strong cultures are led with consistency and courage. Leaders align their own behavior with the organization's declared values. They own the hard decisions and admit when those decisions fall short. They understand that culture is shaped far more by what people observe than by what people are told.

One executive I worked with understood this deeply. Her organization was struggling with burnout, and the culture was tilting toward urgency over thoughtfulness. Instead of launching a wellness campaign, she began leaving the office at 5 p.m. sharp and encouraged her senior team to do the same. Within a month, meeting times shifted, response expectations calmed, and staff energy returned. She didn't need a campaign. She needed credibility, and she earned it through behavior.

Strong culture requires leaders who do not hide behind policies. They step forward to personalize the culture, to live it out loud. They ask hard questions like:

- Where am I misaligned with the culture I say I support?
- How do I model the values in moments of pressure?
- Do my direct reports feel safe to challenge me?
- When people watch me lead, what do they believe this organization actually values?

The answer to those questions determines whether the culture strengthens or fractures.

In weak cultures, leadership sends mixed signals. Accountability may apply to employees, but not to executives. Integrity is expected on paper but ignored for high performers. Leaders show up differently depending on who is watching. In those environments, culture becomes a game of interpretation, not a source of inspiration.

In strong cultures, leadership is steady and human. Leaders do not have to be perfect. They have to be consistent. And when they mess up, and they will, they repair visibly. That vulnerability, when grounded in integrity, builds even more trust than perfection ever could.

Leaders also set the tone for how the organization handles growth. Will the culture scale with it? Will new voices be shaped by the best of the old, or infected by the unresolved contradictions? It is the leader's job to steward not just results, but identity. Because in every organization, culture follows character, and the most watched character is always leadership.

Development Within Strong Cultures

I remember sitting in a strategy session with a corporate CHRO who had just rolled out a new leadership competency model. It looked great on paper. Color-coded. Research-backed. But after two months, no one was using it. Managers weren't referencing it in reviews, leaders weren't modeling it in meetings, and employees had already forgotten the language. Why? Because it was development in theory, not in culture. It hadn't been internalized.

In strong cultures, development is not a program or a quarterly event. It is part of the oxygen. People are growing because the culture expects them to grow, supports their growth, and makes development visible in how work gets done.

Strong cultures teach the unspoken rules. They don't assume people will just absorb what matters. They make the invisible visible. New employees are not left to decode norms through mistakes. Instead, the culture is socialized deliberately, through onboarding rituals, shared stories, modeling by peers, and intentional mentoring. The message is clear: "Here is how we move, here is how we make decisions, here is how we disagree, and here is what it means to belong here."

And it doesn't stop after onboarding. In strong cultures, feedback is frequent and safe. It is normalized, not weaponized. Coaching is not reserved for high-potential talent or performance issues. It is embedded in conversations, team check-ins, peer reflections, and leader 1-on-1s. The message is not just, "You need to grow." The message is, "We all do, and here's how I'll help."

Strong cultures also embed development inside the work itself. Learning is not outsourced to the classroom. It happens in the project, in the conflict, in the customer issue. People are stretched intentionally, not left to sink or swim. They're trusted with stretch assignments, rotated across functions, paired with peers from different teams, and expected to learn through doing.

But what really separates strong culture from shallow development efforts is this: they measure cultural development, not just technical growth. A weak culture tracks how many people completed training. A strong culture asks, "What changed in behavior because of that training?" A weak culture asks if a manager improved team productivity. A strong culture asks if that manager strengthened trust, deepened values alignment, and grew others into better culture carriers.

So how do strong cultures measure development in a meaningful way?

Cultural Maturity Assessments

These go beyond 360s. They assess how well a person embodies and reproduces the organization's core values through their decision-making, conflict style, hiring practices, and cross-functional influence.

Behavioral Indicators

Teams are observed not just for output, but for behavior patterns. Are people giving feedback more constructively? Are psychological safety and inclusion increasing? Are values being invoked in decision points, not just laminated on the wall?

Culture Pulse Checks

Surveys are run not just to get satisfaction scores, but to assess how aligned employees feel with the organization's cultural direction. These are repeated regularly to track not just morale, but maturity.

Development Impact Reviews

Instead of just asking "what skills did you gain," leaders ask "how did this growth help the team operate more culturally aligned?" and "how did it advance the mission, not just the metrics?"

And one of the most powerful signals is who gets promoted and why. In strong cultures, growth is rewarded when it strengthens the whole. Promotions are not just about individual performance. They become celebrations of people who have grown themselves while growing others and embedding culture as they lead.

Strong cultures also see development as a continuous journey. There is no arrival. Culture isn't static, and neither is your growth. As the strategy shifts, as the market changes, as new voices join the table, development ensures the culture doesn't freeze in time. It breathes, expands, and deepens through the people.

When development is cultural, not just technical, you don't just grow better employees. You grow culture keepers. People who model, mentor, and multiply the very thing that makes your organization distinct.

Rewards: What Gets Repeated Gets Reinforced

One of the fastest ways to decode a culture is to ask, "What gets rewarded here?" Not what gets talked about, not what's written in the values deck—but what actually earns praise, bonuses, visibility, access, and advancement. Because people will always chase what gets rewarded. In that way, rewards are not just a tool of culture. They are the loudest form of cultural instruction.

In weak cultures, rewards are disconnected from stated values. An organization says it values collaboration but gives raises only to individual top performers. A civic agency claims to prioritize equity, but promotes only those who maintain the status quo. A nonprofit preaches community, but celebrates heroes. The result? Mixed signals, cultural fatigue, and behavior driven by politics over principle.

In strong cultures, rewards are used to teach, align, and reinforce. They are not afterthoughts. They are strategic.

First, strong cultures reward behaviors as much as results. They do not tolerate high performers who erode trust or violate values. They know that a misaligned high performer is more dangerous than a poor performer, because their success gives permission. Strong cultures ask, "How did they get the result?" not just "Did they hit the number?"

They make the culture visible through who gets spotlighted. That might mean recognizing the teammate who showed resilience under pressure. Or promoting the leader who mentored others into excellence. Or doubling down on the unit that met targets while strengthening inclusion.

Second, strong cultures design systems of recognition that match their values. For example:

- If collaboration is core, then rewards are team-based, not just individual.
- If innovation is prized, then failure that leads to learning is celebrated, not punished.
- If integrity matters, then transparency is rewarded, even when it slows things down.

This doesn't always mean money. Recognition is also about who gets seen and heard. Who gets airtime in meetings? Who is asked to lead big initiatives? Who is invited to strategy tables? These are forms of reward. And every reward teaches the culture what matters.

One organization I worked with had a beautiful value called "shared ownership." But every reward system was built on internal competition. Individual sales rankings. Star performers. "Most Valuable Employee" awards. And they couldn't understand why teams kept withholding information. The answer was simple: the rewards were undermining the stated value. They weren't rewarding ownership. They were rewarding isolation.

Strong cultures align their formal systems with their informal signals. Performance evaluations reference core behaviors. Promotions are earned not just for delivery, but for demonstration of cultural alignment. Incentives are built around reinforcing the operating norms they want to sustain.

They also create rituals of recognition. This may be as simple as shoutouts in team meetings or as structured as a cross-functional peer-nomination system. What matters is that appreciation becomes a daily rhythm, not a quarterly checklist. Because what gets recognized gets repeated.

Measuring the Cultural Impact of Rewards

Strong cultures don't just hand out rewards, they track what happens next. They ask: Did the recognition reinforce alignment? Did it strengthen the behaviors we want more of? Did it accelerate belonging, engagement, and trust?

Here are a few ways strong cultures measure the impact of rewards:

Behavioral Shift Analysis

Are we seeing more of the desired behaviors in teams where recognition has been implemented? For example, if a team recognizes collaboration weekly, are cross-functional partnerships increasing?

Promotion Pattern Review

Who is getting promoted and why? Are those individuals expanding the culture or just repeating their own performance?

Pulse Surveys with Reflection Items

These go beyond 360s. They assess how well a person embodies and reproduces the organization's core values through their decision-making, conflict style, hiring practices, and cross-functional influence.

Peer Feedback Loops

After formal recognition, do peers report increased trust or psychological safety with that individual? Do others express motivation to adopt similar behaviors?

Turnover Analysis

Are high-value employees staying or leaving based on perceived fairness and consistency in recognition and rewards? Disengagement due to misaligned reward systems is a silent but powerful drain.

Engagement Indexing

Does the volume and quality of recognition correlate with employee engagement scores, innovation metrics, or resilience under pressure?

None of this is about micromanaging appreciation. It is about auditing whether your culture is actually reinforcing what you say you value. If the answer is unclear, your culture is being shaped by default—not design.

Finally, strong cultures reward not just outcomes, but cultural stewardship. The people who mentor, who model, who coach, who challenge norms respectfully. These are the culture keepers. And when they are seen and celebrated, they multiply.

If you want to know what your culture really values, look at who gets promoted, protected, and praised. And if you want to change your culture, start changing what you reward—and start measuring what that reward produces.

Accountability: The Backbone of Credibility

If relationships are the social glue and leadership is the compass, accountability is the backbone. Without it, even the most inspiring culture collapses under the weight of contradiction. Accountability is what makes values real. It is where alignment either shows up or disappears.

I once worked with a large nonprofit where inclusion was written on every wall and website. But when I asked frontline staff if they felt safe speaking up, I heard silence. Not because people didn't care. Because nothing happened when issues were raised. Or worse, retaliation followed. The organization had values—but no accountability. So the values meant nothing.

In a strong culture, accountability is not punishment. It is alignment. It is how the organization maintains integrity. It is the difference between aspirational words and actual expectations. Without it, you create cultural dissonance. People hear one thing and see another. That gap—between stated culture and lived reality—is where trust dies.

Strong cultures don't just expect performance. They expect integrity, follow-through, and cultural contribution. They hold people accountable for how results are achieved, not just whether numbers are hit. And they apply that accountability consistently across roles, ranks, and relationships.

Here's what that looks like:

- Leaders don't get special passes. If a senior executive undermines the culture, they are confronted, coached, or removed—just like anyone else. Because in strong cultures, no one is culturally exempt.
- Culture violations are addressed, not ignored. If someone dominates conversations in a culture that values inclusion, that gets named. If someone hoards information in a culture of collaboration, that gets confronted.
- Accountability is real-time and relational. It doesn't wait for annual reviews. It happens through regular feedback, clear boundaries, and mutual expectation-setting.

Strong cultures make accountability part of the norm, not a threat. It's not a trapdoor that people fall through when they mess up. It's a set of handrails people use to stay on track. Everyone knows what behavior is expected. Everyone knows how it's addressed when misalignment happens. That clarity creates safety, not fear.

In these environments, accountability becomes a form of care. When we care about people, we don't let them veer off course silently. We bring them back. We offer feedback with respect. We set high standards because we believe in their ability to meet them.

Accountability also ensures consequences are connected to culture. If someone violates trust, the consequence is not arbitrary, it's a cultural correction. It protects the integrity of the group. And it sends a clear message: "This culture matters, and we will uphold it together."

Too often, organizations confuse accountability with conflict. So they avoid it. They let misaligned behavior fester. They protect high performers because they're afraid of the short-term fallout. But long-term, that fear erodes everything. Because people aren't just watching the misalignment. They're watching whether you'll address it.

Strong cultures handle accountability with maturity. They use clear frameworks for feedback, coaching plans that include cultural alignment, and shared norms for calling people in rather than just calling them out. They expect accountability to be modeled at the top and practiced throughout.

And yes, they measure it too.

- Are misalignments addressed promptly?
- Do people believe accountability is fair and consistent?
- Are leaders modeling corrective behavior or just talking about it?
- Is there a shared language for calling attention to cultural drift?

In the absence of accountability, culture becomes a performance. In the presence of accountability, culture becomes a way of life.

Because at the end of the day, if you're not willing to hold people accountable for the culture—you don't have one.

Branding as a Cultural Seal

I was once called in by a fast-scaling tech nonprofit whose brand had taken off faster than its infrastructure. Donors loved them. Media outlets were profiling them. Their visuals were slick, and their website beamed with values like equity, creativity, and community. But inside the organization? Burnout was high, turnover was rising, and employees whispered that the culture was anything but equitable or creative. What they had was a brand, but not a cultural seal. And the dissonance was starting to show.

Brand is not what you say. It is who you are on your worst day.

In a strong culture, branding is not a veneer, it's a mirror. The brand reflects the reality of how people treat each other, make decisions, and live out values, not just what the marketing team produces. In other words, your external image is a direct extension of your internal consistency.

Strong cultures don't brand their values. They behave them. And because the behavior is consistent, it becomes the brand.

Take Patagonia. Their stance on environmental responsibility doesn't just show up in ads. It shows up in supply chain decisions, legal battles, customer engagement, even in telling people not to buy new gear. The brand is credible because it's culturally aligned. That's the seal. It cannot be faked.

In weak cultures, branding becomes a substitute for culture. A beautifully crafted DEI statement is published while pay equity remains unaddressed. A "people-first" tagline gets printed on coffee mugs while exit interviews reveal toxicity. That gap erodes both reputation and retention. Because eventually, the public catches up to the private reality.

In strong cultures, branding is built on alignment—not just with values, but across all modes of communication. Whether digital, visual, verbal, or experiential, the same cultural tone comes through.

- The website sounds like the actual voices inside the organization.
- Social media reflects the kind of energy you'd feel walking the halls.
- Public statements don't need spin, because they come from cultural truth.

And storytelling is central. Stories are how cultures preserve identity and transmit belief. Strong cultures are intentional about which stories they tell. They highlight stories that reinforce shared values, showcase cultural stewards, and remind people why they belong. These stories become more than content—they become cultural currency.

Symbols matter too. Whether it's the design of your logo, the names of your conference rooms, or the artifacts you display at events, these signals either reinforce or confuse your culture. A community-centered nonprofit that names all meeting rooms after donors may send a very different cultural message than it intends. A faith-based health organization that never references its faith in external messaging creates a perception gap that undermines trust from both staff and community.

Strong cultures are not afraid to reject what doesn't fit. That includes marketing trends, partnerships, or even media exposure that misrepresents who they truly are. Culture is the filter. If a flashy campaign distorts the values, they'll pull it. Because consistency beats applause.

They also check for internal and external alignment. Ask anyone who works there, "Does the brand feel true to what it's like inside?" If you hear hesitation or disclaimers, there's a breach. If you hear, "Exactly," or better yet, "Yes, and more," you've got a cultural seal.

Finally, branding becomes a diagnostic tool for strong cultures. They watch how their people talk about the organization when no one is prompting them. They read Glassdoor reviews for patterns, not ego. They listen to customer conversations and ask, "Does this sound like who we are?" If not, they don't just fix the brand. They fix the culture.

Because in the end, branding is not about storytelling. It's about story keeping. When your people can keep the story alive without scripts or slide decks—when they live it naturally, speak it fluently, and defend it instinctively—you don't just have a brand. You have a culture that seals itself.

The Spectrum of Cultural Intensity

In a recent session with a board of directors, I asked a simple but disorienting question: "How strong do you want your culture to be?" They looked confused. "We want a good culture," someone said. "A positive one." But strength isn't the same as goodness. Strength is about clarity, consistency, and intensity. And that's where most leaders hesitate—because they haven't wrestled with just how strong they want their culture to be, or what that strength costs.

Not every strong culture is the same. Cultures, like personalities, operate at different intensities. Some are loud, demanding, all-in. Others are steady, balanced, more human-centered. Others are loose, open, and flexible. None of these are inherently better. But what is dangerous is unintentional intensity—when your culture is stronger or weaker than you realize, and no one is managing the consequences.

Let's break it down.

High-Intensity Cultures: Power and Risk

These are cultures where everything is tightly held and strongly expressed. Expectations are exact. Feedback is frequent. Norms are sacred. Belonging is earned through alignment and performance. You know you're in a high-intensity culture when you feel it in your body—people move faster, speak with conviction, and have no doubt about what's acceptable.

Think of elite sports organizations, global consulting firms, some high-growth tech startups, or legacy faith institutions. These cultures create immense clarity, loyalty, and performance—but they also carry weight. The tradeoffs include burnout risk, low psychological safety for dissenters, and barriers to diversity of thought. These cultures are not for everyone—and that's often by design.

Balanced-Intensity Cultures: Sustainability and Adaptability

These cultures still have clarity, but with room to breathe. They reward values, not just velocity. Feedback is present but developmental. Power is shared and structured. The culture is strong, but flexible. You know what's expected, and you also know how to challenge or evolve it.

Think of mature purpose-driven companies, resilient civic institutions, or nonprofits that balance mission with reflection. These cultures build endurance. They attract talent that wants clarity and care. They may move more slowly than high-intensity cultures, but they recover faster from setbacks and often retain institutional memory better.

Relaxed-Intensity Cultures: Autonomy and Inclusion

At this end of the spectrum, cultures are shaped more by freedom than enforcement. Guidelines exist, but there's wide latitude in how people interpret and express them. Trust is given early. People are expected to self-manage. Rules are fewer. Hierarchy is less visible.

You'll find this in creative firms, open-source movements, flat organizations, or startups still forming their identity. These cultures feel inviting, informal, and adaptive, but they can also drift. Without strong anchors, inconsistency can sneak in. Some people thrive here. Others flounder. The risk is cultural erosion if no one is naming the patterns.

There Is No Right Answer—Only Deliberate Fit

Strong culture does not mean high-intensity. In fact, the strongest cultures are not necessarily the loudest. They are simply the clearest, most consistent, and best aligned with their purpose.

Intensity must match your mission, your people, and your strategic context. A trauma center requires different cultural intensity than a mentoring nonprofit. A startup disrupting an industry may need rigor that would exhaust a university system. What matters is being honest about what kind of strength you need, and what kind of strength your people can sustain.

Managing Tradeoffs and Warning Signs

With high intensity, watch for exhaustion, exclusion, and conformity over creativity.

With balanced intensity, guard against complacency or masking of conflict.

With relaxed intensity, be alert to drift, inconsistency, and unmet accountability.

Strong cultures are not blind to these risks. They manage the tension. They build in release valves, feedback loops, and reflection spaces. They adjust intensity with intention, not as a reaction to crisis, but as a rhythm of resilience.

Examples Across the Spectrum

- Amazon operates at a high-intensity level: customer obsession, relentless drive, and internal competition. It attracts a specific type of contributor.
- Chick-fil-A represents a balanced-intensity culture: clarity of service standards, deep values, and consistent family ethos.
- IDEO thrives on relaxed-intensity: creative freedom, fluid teams, and a premium on openness and trust.

Each is strong. Each has edges. But what they share is a deliberate definition of how strong they want to be—and systems to hold it.

Summary

By now, you've seen that culture is not soft. It is not the poster on the wall or the HR initiative that fades. It is the real system underneath every conversation, every conflict, every decision, and every outcome.

Culture is not what you say about yourself. It is what others experience through you.

Culture is not what you aspire to. It's what you allow, what you repeat, what you protect.

Strong culture is not about control. It's about coherence. It gives people something solid to stand on, and something meaningful to stand for. It builds loyalty without coercion. It creates alignment without uniformity. It fosters innovation without chaos.

And most importantly, strong culture gives you the power to scale without losing your soul.

When you define what strength means for you, and when you commit to living it every day, culture doesn't become one more thing to manage. It becomes the very thing that makes everything else possible.

Strong culture is the foundation. The work ahead is to build on it with intention. Leaders do not stumble into coherence. They design for it. They make choices about what to reward, what to correct, and what to fund so that the culture people feel matches the values leaders preach.

So, the question shifts from what culture is to how you will architect it. How will you translate conviction into systems? How will you turn values into visible behaviors? How will you align decisions, incentives, and daily rhythms so that culture shows up when the pressure does?

That is where we go next. From definition to design. From inspiration to integration. From a clear picture of strength to a practical roadmap for building it on purpose.

CHAPTER 4

INTENTIONALLY CREATING CULTURE
BUILDING A ROADMAP AND MASTER PLAN

I sat with a CEO recently who said to me, "I think our culture's good... people like working here." I nodded, then asked, "So what happens when performance tanks and you have to cut perks? What holds the center then?" His smile faded. Culture isn't about comfort. It's about conviction.

Building a strong and intentional culture isn't a communications exercise or a branding refresh. It's a deliberate act of leadership. It's planning with courage, following through with consistency, and paying attention to the hard trade-offs. As we explored in Chapter 3, culture is not what follows success. It is what allows it.

And the strength of that culture? It doesn't lie in having the "right" values but in how predictably people live by your values. Whether you sit in the C-suite or lead a portfolio of programs, your role is to embed culture not only in vision decks but in decisions, incentives, structures, and day-to-day behaviors.

This chapter is your step-by-step roadmap—designed to help you architect, operationalize, and sustain a culture that is not only meaningful but also aligned with your business strategy and stakeholder expectations.

Be Honest: What Price Are You Willing to Pay?

Here's the first truth: culture transformation will cost you something. Time, money, energy, control, even relationships. Leaders often start strong, but when the cost becomes real—when it's time to hold a high performer accountable or say no to a lucrative opportunity that violates your values—the vision can shrink.

So before you begin, ask yourself and your leadership team:

- Are we willing to make tough decisions that align with our cultural priorities?
- How much autonomy will we give employees to maintain our culture?
- Are we prepared to let go of employees or leaders who don't align with cultural vision?
- Will we prioritize long-term culture health over short-term profits?

In Chapter 3, we said that the opposite of a strong culture is not toxicity. It's ambiguity. And ambiguity thrives when leaders are unwilling to pay the price for clarity. Strong cultures do not happen by inspiration alone. They require sustained investment—in governance, leadership modeling, real feedback loops, and accountability systems that don't blink when things get uncomfortable.

We will now jump into a rigorous roadmap and master plan for creating a strong culture. The goal is for you to answer all the questions for your organization. Customize as you desire to reach your organization's desired strong culture and goals.

Phase One: Define the Cultural DNA

Step 1: Identifying and Prioritizing Stakeholders

In every culture initiative I've led, one question always emerges early: "Who are we doing this for?" That question reveals everything. Because defining culture in isolation from the people it's meant to serve—internal and external—always leads to disconnection.

Culture alignment starts by naming your ecosystem. The behaviors you want to see must make sense not only to your employees but also to your board, your customers, your regulators, your community. Culture is a networked asset.

Key Stakeholder Groups

- **Internal:** Employees, leadership, board of directors
- **External:** Customers, investors, community partners, regulators

Action Items

1. Conduct stakeholder mapping to identify who influences culture most. Treat this as a systems-level view. Who holds the real levers of influence, directly or indirectly?
2. Define stakeholder priorities and expectations. Clarify what each group cares about and expects from your organization's culture—where values align, and where there's potential friction.
3. Establish a feedback loop for ongoing stakeholder input. Culture is alive. That means what people expect from it will evolve. You need a way to stay tuned in.
4. Create engagement mechanisms so stakeholders aren't just consulted, but also invested in the outcome. That includes structured conversations, participation opportunities, and visibility into how their input is shaping outcomes.

Deliverables

- Stakeholder Mapping and Prioritization Matrix: A visual snapshot of who matters most to culture and why.
- Stakeholder Engagement Strategy: A game plan for involving each group, with clarity on when, how, and to what end.
- Feedback Mechanism Documentation: Systems for gathering and using input—not once, but continuously.
- Communication Channel Framework: A map of how culture-related messages flow across relationships and platforms.

Estimated Time: 2–3 weeks

Step 2: Laying the Foundation: Purpose, Values, and Mission

Culture begins with what you believe, but it becomes real when it shapes what you build. Purpose is not a tagline. It's a blueprint. Every strong culture I've seen has one thing in common—unshakable clarity on why the organization exists, what it values, and where it's going.

Don't skip this. Even if you've done it before, revisit it now. Alignment starts with shared understanding.

Key Elements

- **Vision:** Where are we going?
- **Mission:** Why do we exist?
- **Core Values:** What non-negotiables guide how we act?

Action Items

1. Host executive alignment sessions to finalize the vision, mission, and values. Don't assume agreement—facilitate it.
2. Develop a communication strategy that doesn't just tell people the values but helps them internalize them.
3. Align statements with business strategy and operational goals. Purpose without execution is poetry.
4. Create implementation guidelines for each value. Make the invisible visible. What does this value look like on a Tuesday in Q4?

Deliverables

- Finalized Vision, Mission, and Values Document: Aligned, signed off, and ready to cascade.
- Communication and Engagement Plan: A multi-layered approach to help employees understand, own, and live the culture.
- Implementation Guidelines: Specifics on how values show up in practice across functions.
- Alignment Documentation: Clear evidence that culture is not a separate initiative but embedded in strategy.

Estimated Time: 3–4 weeks

Step 3: Define the Culture Vision

This is where you paint the picture. Culture Vision is not just a statement, it's a vivid snapshot of the future you're building—seen through behaviors, language, and daily choices. It connects aspiration with execution.

This is how you answer the unspoken question employees ask every day: "What kind of place is this?"

Action Items

1. Create a written Culture Vision Statement that spells out tangible behaviors and expectations. It should feel actionable, not abstract.
2. Ensure leadership models the Culture Vision daily. Your leaders are the culture. People don't believe what they hear, they believe what they see.
3. Use storytelling and case studies to make it real. Show, don't just tell. Bring the values to life with examples that stick.
4. Develop measurement criteria for how well the vision is being lived. You can't improve what you don't measure.
5. Create feedback mechanisms to make sure the vision is clear, relevant, and understood at all levels.
6. Design reinforcement systems that recognize and reward culture-aligned behavior. Every system either strengthens or sabotages culture. Make sure yours strengthens it.

Deliverables

- Culture Vision Statement with Behavioral Anchors: Not just what we believe, but how we behave.
- Leadership Modeling Guidelines: Coaching tools and examples for how leaders can walk the talk.
- Story Bank and Case Study Collection: Real stories of the culture in action—used in onboarding, training, and town halls.
- Vision Alignment Measurement Framework: A dashboard of metrics and insights that tell you how well the culture is working.
- Feedback System Documentation: Clear channels for input that keep the vision evolving with your organization.
- Reinforcement Strategy Documentation: Programs that celebrate and reward culture carriers—the people who model the vision every day.

Estimated Time: 3–4 weeks

Step 4: Determine Your Current Cultural Positioning on the Strength Spectrum

Here's where the diagnostic begins. Once you've finalized your working definitions and context for culture, it's time to define where your culture currently stands—and how it shows up—in a consistent, measurable way. We use a Cultural Strength Spectrum, and it's intentionally behavioral. No fluff, no vague values that could mean anything to anyone. This is about what people actually see and experience every day.

The Cultural Strength Spectrum measures the strength of each behavior in your current culture against the desired future state. It gives you a baseline of where you are so you can decide what to keep, shift, or redesign. This spectrum runs from Weak to Strong, with "Intentional" being the goal—not perfect, not idealistic, but deliberately defined, aligned, and supported across the system.

Each behavior is rated along this strength spectrum:

- **Weak:** Inconsistent, unclear, often damaging, eroding trust or performance.
- **Emerging:** Some pockets of clarity or good practice, but not reinforced or sustainable.
- **Functional:** Works for now, supports basic operations, but not strategic or differentiating.
- **Strong:** Consistently reinforced, supports strategy, attracts and retains talent.
- **Intentional:** Co-created, measured, and adaptive. Integrated across systems and leadership. Designed to evolve.

You can use any tool that maps culture behaviorally. Ours is built on 21 behavioral dimensions grouped into four domains:

DOMAIN A: Strategic Foundation

These dimensions reflect the core beliefs and orientation of how the organization sees the world and frames its strategy.

- **Risk Tolerance**—How much ambiguity, failure, or experimentation is culturally acceptable
- **Power Distance**—How authority is distributed and decisions are made across levels
- **Task vs. Relationship Orientation**—The balance between getting results and maintaining harmony
- **Time Orientation**—Short-term wins vs. long-term investments
- **Change Readiness**—Willingness to adapt, transform, or unlearn
- **Purpose Clarity**—How well the organization and its people understand and live the 'why' behind their work

DOMAIN B: Operational Approach

These behaviors influence how work flows and how decisions get executed.

7. Decision-Making—Centralized or distributed, data-driven or instinctual
8. Collaboration Style—Siloed, cooperative, integrated, or co-owned
9. Communication—Direct or indirect, transparent or guarded, frequency and cadence
10. Process Orientation—Rigid, flexible, optimized, or chaotic
11. Knowledge Management—How information is shared, stored, and reused

DOMAIN C: People Management

These behaviors shape the experience of employees and how leaders invest in their people.

12. Learning Approach—Formal vs. informal, structured vs. ad hoc
13. Performance Recognition—What gets rewarded and how
14. Employee Development—Coaching, training, mentoring, and support for growth
15. Work-Life Integration—Expectations around boundaries, flexibility, and balance
16. Career Progression—How advancement is defined, supported, and perceived

DOMAIN D: External Engagement

These behaviors reflect how the organization shows up beyond its walls—with customers, partners, and communities.

17. Customer Orientation–Reactive or proactive, transactional or relational
18. Innovation Approach–Incremental vs. disruptive, internal vs. open
19. Community Impact–Commitment to social good, sustainability, and equity
20. Partnership Style–Control vs. trust-based alliances
21. Market Positioning–Conservative follower or bold differentiator

Once you assess each of the 21 dimensions across this spectrum, you'll begin to see clear patterns. Those patterns form the current cultural signature of your organization—not just what's written on the walls or in the handbook, but what people actually feel and live.

What's Next?

From here, you'll identify what needs to shift, and in which order, based on alignment to your strategy, gaps in your operating model, or tensions showing up across teams. But naming it—behaviorally, honestly, and with systems-wide visibility—is the first act of leadership.

Take your time. This step is not about quick fixes. It's about seeing clearly so you can lead courageously.

Step 4 Deliverables and Action Items

Action Items

1. **Assess current positioning across all dimensions**

    Establish a baseline for the organization's cultural state. Identify where it's thriving, where it's drifting, and where it may be fractured.

2. **Define desired positioning for each dimension**

    Clarify where you want the organization to be. This isn't about perfection—it's about intentionality aligned with strategy and values.

3. **Create transition plans for any desired shifts**

    Design roadmaps to move from current to desired culture. Specify actions, owners, and sequencing that makes the transformation real, not rhetorical

4. **Develop measurement criteria for each dimension**

    Culture can't just be felt. You have to track it. Establish metrics and observation methods to measure movement and reinforce accountability.

5. **Design decision-making frameworks that reinforce positioning**

    Culture shows up in choices. Help leaders make decisions that align with your intentional positioning—especially when it's inconvenient.

6. **Establish monitoring mechanisms for cultural consistency**

    Sustainability isn't automatic. Create feedback loops to catch drift early, reinforce what's working, and course correct what's not.

Deliverables

- **Cultural Positioning Assessment Report**

    Detailed analysis of where the organization currently stands across all 21 dimensions. Your cultural X-ray.

- **Future State Definition Document**

    Strategic blueprint for where you want to be. This outlines desired positioning on each dimension and the reasons behind each one.

- **Transition Roadmap and Timeline**

    Clear project plan with owners, actions, and deadlines to get from now to next.

- **Measurement Criteria Documentation**

    List of indicators, signals, and performance metrics to track cultural progress over time.

- **Decision-Making Frameworks**

    Tools and examples that help leaders make choices aligned with the intended culture in real-world scenarios.

- **Monitoring System Documentation**

    Practical process for ongoing tracking, including pulse checks, team huddles, and review mechanisms.

Estimated Time: 4–5 weeks

Step 5: Building Blocks—Rituals, Traditions, and Shared Language

In Chapter 3, we talked about how culture isn't just what you say, it's what you repeat. In this step, we move from behavioral positioning to daily expression—rituals, traditions, and language that either make or break the credibility of your culture.

Strong cultures build memory. They embed meaning into behavior. And they teach people how to belong without having to ask. Whether you're leading a Fortune 500 or a fast-moving nonprofit, this is where culture becomes sticky and alive.

Core Elements

- Rituals strengthen identity through regular practices

    Daily stand-ups, Monday wins, quarterly roundtables—these rhythms set the tone and expectation.

- Traditions reinforce company values

    Founder's Day, onboarding letters, exit messages, culture coins—small symbolic acts that carry big cultural weight.

- Shared language ensures consistency in how culture is communicated and understood

    What we call customers, what we name our values, even how we label mistakes—language signals truth.

Action Items

1. **Establish rituals that embed cultural values into everyday work**

   Design intentional rhythms across teams and functions. Don't just let routines evolve—shape them.

2. **Document shared language in internal communications and training**

   Build a reference so everyone speaks the same language, no matter their role or region.

3. **Create cultural celebration frameworks**

   Tie recognition to values. Don't just say "good job"—say why it matters and how it connects to the culture you're building.

4. **Design recognition ceremonies**

   Use moments of public visibility to reinforce behaviors and elevate cultural exemplars.

5. **Develop storytelling guidelines**

   Teach leaders how to tell the stories that carry meaning. Create a cadence and format that makes sharing easy and powerful.

Deliverables

- **Ritual and Tradition Playbook**

    Practical catalog of recommended rituals and traditions tied to the organization's purpose and values.

- **Cultural Language Guide**

    Glossary of key terms and cultural phrases to be used consistently in training, communication, and leadership moments.

- **Celebration Framework**

    Blueprint for how to celebrate wins and behaviors in ways that reinforce desired culture.

- **Recognition Program Documentation**

    Process and criteria for formally recognizing individuals or teams aligned with cultural values.

- **Storytelling Guidelines and Templates**

    Tools that help leaders shape and share stories that reflect the soul of the organization.

Estimated Time: 6–8 weeks

Step 6: Align Capital and Resource Allocation with Culture

When I sat with the COO of a fast-scaling healthcare network, we discovered something telling. They had all the right language around inclusion, empowerment, and innovation—but when we reviewed their budgets, those priorities were nowhere to be found. Not in leadership development, not in incentives, not in how they measured performance. Culture doesn't live in mission statements. It lives in where the money goes.

As we explored in Chapter 3, strong cultures demonstrate their values not just through words, but through how they allocate their resources. This alignment between capital and values creates credibility, clarity, and consistent cultural expression across the organization.

Culture is not free. It requires financial and structural investment. Resource allocation must match the behaviors and beliefs the organization wants to scale. That means leadership development must reinforce cultural expectations. Compensation must reward aligned behaviors. Engagement efforts must be funded, not just encouraged.

When organizations fail to align their spending with their stated values, they create a dangerous cultural dissonance. People stop believing in the message. And eventually, they stop living it.

Action Items

1. **Analyze current resource allocation patterns against cultural priorities**

    Reveal misalignments between what the organization says it values and where it actually spends.

2. **Allocate budget for culture-building initiatives**

    Dedicate financial resources to programs that embody cultural values—don't rely on volunteerism or side-of-desk energy.

3. **Ensure reward systems incentivize cultural alignment**

    Align recognition, bonuses, promotions, and evaluations with specific cultural behaviors, not just business outcomes.

4. **Create investment frameworks that support cultural goals**

    Build decision tools that integrate cultural priorities into capital planning and operational funding decisions.

5. **Develop monitoring systems for resource alignment**

   Track resource allocation against culture to ensure sustained focus and agility when priorities shift.

6. **Establish regular review processes for cultural investments**

   Evaluate ROI of culture-focused expenditures using both quantitative impact and qualitative insight.

Deliverables

- **Resource Allocation Framework**

  Guides how financial and human capital are distributed to support culture. Defines criteria for decision-making and prioritization.

- **Cultural Investment Plan**

  Outlines specific allocations for cultural programs, timelines for implementation, and expected results.

- **Reward System Documentation**

  Clarifies how compensation, promotions, and recognition are linked to culture, ensuring consistent application.

- **Investment Monitoring Tools**

  Provides real-time data dashboards and analytics that track cultural ROI and allocation effectiveness.

- **Review Process Guidelines**

  Structures how and when cultural investments are evaluated, with clear metrics and governance.

- **Alignment Assessment Tools**

  Enables diagnosis of resource-to-culture alignment gaps and offers targeted strategies to close them.

Estimated Time: 6–8 weeks

Phase Three: Sustain and Strengthen Culture

Step 7: Courage and Honesty in Leadership

I once coached a Senior VP in a global logistics firm who privately admitted, "We say people first, but I'm afraid to speak up when decisions contradict that." The problem wasn't values—it was silence. Cultures grow when leaders act with courage and speak with honesty. Without those two, even strong values rot.

As demonstrated in Chapter 3, leaders shape culture most powerfully through behavior. And no behavior is more culturally defining than the decision to tell the truth and take bold action when it matters most.

This is about far more than individual integrity. It's about creating systems that support leaders when they're faced with tough, values-based decisions—and cultures that expect transparent communication. Trust is built when leaders show they're willing to say what's hard and do what's right.

Action Items

1. **Train leaders in courageous conversations and decision-making**

    Equip leaders to address tension head-on, make hard calls, and navigate backlash with integrity.

2. **Establish transparent feedback mechanisms for cultural accountability**

    Create channels where employees can safely flag cultural misalignments or gaps between words and action.

3. **Create leadership development programs focused on cultural stewardship**

    Embed cultural expectations into leadership learning journeys at all levels of the organization.

4. **Design systems for honest communication and feedback**

    Foster psychological safety through communication protocols, listening systems, and trusted feedback loops.

5. **Develop support structures for difficult cultural decisions**

   Provide coaching, ethics resources, and advisory support for leaders navigating tough cultural crossroads.

6. **Implement regular cultural alignment check-ins**

   Set up structured rhythms for leaders to reflect on and re-ground themselves in cultural priorities.

Deliverables

- **Leadership Training Curriculum**

  Develops capacity for courage, clarity, and alignment in decision-making and interpersonal leadership.

- **Feedback System Documentation**

  Lays out how employees provide input, how it's reviewed, and how follow-up action is tracked.

- **Development Program Framework**

  Defines learning objectives and development pathways for cultural leadership across all levels.

- **Communication Guidelines**

  Offers tools, language, and principles for honest conversations and values-based dialogue.

- **Decision Support Tools**

  Guides for ethical dilemmas and complex decisions, built around organizational values.

- **Cultural Alignment Checklist**

  Practical tool to evaluate leadership actions, initiatives, and decisions against the organization's cultural standards.

Estimated Time: 8–10 weeks

Step 8: Consistency in Reinforcement

One of my clients, a Deputy Commissioner for a federal agency, sat across from me in quiet frustration. "I know what we want the culture to be. We've said it. We've published it. But it's like no one lives it." What she was describing was the most common cultural death trap—declared values with no reinforcement.

As we discussed in Chapter 3, strong cultures don't stay strong by accident. They stay strong because they are reinforced constantly, across every part of the organization. Not just in words, but in systems, rituals, consequences, and rewards. That reinforcement has to live inside daily operations, performance conversations, recognition structures, and ongoing learning. Otherwise, culture fades from a living reality to corporate wallpaper.

A culture that matters is one that's reinforced through every rhythm, interaction, and signal the organization sends. The moment someone gets rewarded for violating the values—or punished for living them—is the moment culture becomes a lie. Consistent reinforcement is the heartbeat of cultural credibility.

Action Items:

1. **Standardize performance metrics for cultural alignment**

    Create formalized criteria that explicitly link performance evaluations to cultural behaviors. This ensures people know that living the values isn't optional—it's how they grow.

2. **Implement consistent reward and recognition programs**

    Design structured systems to highlight and celebrate actions that model the culture. What gets rewarded gets repeated.

3. **Develop ongoing cultural training initiatives**

    Make cultural fluency a continuous journey. New hires need immersion. Veterans need refreshers. Leaders need mastery.

4. **Create systematic reinforcement mechanisms**

    Embed cultural reminders in the flow of work—through checklists, meeting protocols, dashboards, email templates. Keep values top of mind by weaving them into how work gets done.

5. **Design regular cultural celebration events**

   Host meaningful rituals that elevate the culture and celebrate milestones. These aren't just parties—they're public declarations of who you are.

6. **Establish continuous feedback loops**

   Set up channels to gather real-time insights on cultural behavior. Think 360 reviews, culture pulse surveys, town halls with teeth. Listening must lead to action.

Deliverables:

- **Performance Measurement Framework**

  A comprehensive evaluation system outlining how cultural behaviors are assessed alongside performance, including metrics, rating scales, and documentation.

- **Recognition Program Documentation**

  A plan that details criteria and formats for consistently recognizing culture-aligned behaviors across all departments and levels.

- **Training Program Curriculum**

  Structured learning pathways, from onboarding to ongoing development, that deepen understanding and consistent application of cultural principles.

- **Reinforcement System Guidelines**

  Practical tools that embed cultural reminders into workflows, including how-to guides for integrating values into decisions and meetings.

- **Event Planning Templates**

  Plug-and-play formats for hosting cultural celebration events—agendas, recognition scripts, logistics guidance—to ensure every gathering reinforces the culture.

- Feedback System Documentation

    Protocols and platforms for capturing and responding to cultural alignment feedback, creating a rhythm of continuous improvement.

Estimated Time: 6–8 weeks

Phase Four: Evolve & Scale Culture

Step 9: Creating a Shared Identity

I once worked with the leadership team of a growing tech nonprofit that had expanded from 30 to 300 employees in under two years. They were passionate, brilliant, and completely fractured. "We used to be a tribe," the COO said. "Now it feels like a thousand different agendas." That's the moment I knew they didn't just need a culture—they needed a shared identity.

Organizations with strong cultures cultivate an identity that transcends departments, generations, and geography. This identity doesn't come from branding campaigns. It comes from consistency between what you say and what you do—at every level.

Shared identity unites people across difference. It allows an organization to grow without losing itself. It gives employees, customers, and stakeholders something they can feel, belong to, and believe in. When culture shows up consistently at every touchpoint, it becomes more than internal language. It becomes the soul of the organization.

Action Items:

1. **Establish clear external branding that aligns with internal culture**

    Your messaging to the world should reflect the truth of who you are inside. Authenticity builds trust—especially in a skeptical world.

2. **Foster community engagement through shared purpose and corporate responsibility**

    Tie your cultural values to something bigger than the organization. Let your culture breathe beyond profit. Let it serve.

3. **Create mechanisms for cultural expression across all stakeholders**

   Design intentional ways for employees, customers, partners, and investors to all experience the culture in meaningful and consistent ways.

4. **Develop systematic approaches to cultural storytelling**

   Capture the real stories that animate your values. Use them to teach, inspire, and reinforce the culture through emotion and memory.

5. **Design cultural onboarding experiences for new stakeholders**

   From day one, make sure people experience your culture, not just hear about it. The first impression is the cultural imprint.

6. **Build frameworks for maintaining identity through growth**

   Whether scaling, merging, or evolving—have a plan for holding on to what matters most. Culture must be portable and protected.

Deliverables:

- **Brand Alignment Strategy**

  A clear plan for consistent cultural expression across all external communications—messaging, visual identity, tone, and customer experiences.

- **Community Engagement Framework**

  Structured initiatives that tie organizational values to broader societal impact—measuring meaning, not just metrics.

- **Cultural Expression Playbook**

  A guide for how cultural values are lived and communicated across different stakeholder groups, with tools and templates for execution.

- **Storytelling Guidelines and Templates**

  Practical frameworks and examples to help leaders share powerful, authentic stories that embody the culture.

- **Onboarding Experience Design**

    A detailed blueprint for how new employees, customers, and partners are introduced to the culture, including journey maps and messaging flows.

- **Growth Management Toolkit**

    Scalable systems, assessment tools, and decision frameworks for preserving cultural integrity during change, including acquisition integration and global expansion.

Estimated Time: 8–10 weeks

Step 10: Scaling Cultural Systems

Building on Chapter 3's exploration of how strong cultures maintain consistency at scale, organizations must develop systematic approaches to preserving cultural strength through growth and change. This requires creating scalable systems that can maintain cultural consistency while adapting to new contexts and challenges.

Successful scaling requires careful attention to both formal and informal cultural transmission mechanisms. While formal systems provide the framework for cultural consistency, informal networks and relationships play crucial roles in maintaining cultural authenticity during growth. Organizations must build systems that support both aspects while maintaining flexibility for local adaptation.

Action Items:

1. Create scalable cultural training and development programs: Flexible learning systems that transmit core values efficiently using digital platforms and train-the-trainer models.

2. Design adaptation frameworks for different contexts: Structured guidelines that define cultural boundaries while allowing contextual variation.

3. Develop cultural integration processes for new locations or acquisitions: Systematic methods to embed culture in new entities, balancing respect and consistency.

4. Build systems for maintaining consistency across growth: Governance mechanisms like cultural ambassadors and standardized assessments to prevent fragmentation.

5. Establish cultural measurement systems that scale: Tech-enabled, sample-based frameworks for monitoring cultural health without excessive complexity.

6. Create frameworks for local cultural adaptation: Decision tools to determine which elements must remain fixed and which may flex by context.

Deliverables:

- **Scalable Training Program Design:** Blueprint with digital tools, modular content, and trainer certification paths.

- **Adaptation Framework Documentation:** Clear guidance on what can flex versus what must hold across geographies and units.

- **Integration Process Playbook:** Timelines, roles, and metrics for embedding culture in new or acquired parts of the business.

- **Consistency Maintenance Guidelines:** Protocols and practices for preserving alignment amid expansion.

- **Measurement System Design:** Efficient systems for cultural diagnostics across a growing enterprise.

- **Local Adaptation Toolkit:** Templates and frameworks to guide culturally sensitive decisions in new settings.

Estimated Time: 10–12 weeks

Step 11: Evolution Management

As we explored in Chapter 3, strong cultures must balance consistency with the ability to evolve. This step focuses on creating systems that allow for intentional cultural evolution while maintaining cultural strength. Organizations need mechanisms to sense when evolution is needed and processes to manage change while preserving core cultural elements.

Evolution management requires careful attention to both the pace and direction of change. Organizations must develop capabilities to identify necessary cultural shifts, manage the transition process, and maintain cultural strength through periods of change. This requires both systematic approaches to monitoring cultural health and flexible frameworks for managing evolution.

Action Items:

1. Develop cultural evolution sensing mechanisms: Internal and external scans that serve as early warning systems for needed change.

2. Create frameworks for managing cultural change: Practical guidance to plan and execute intentional evolution without disorientation.

3. Build systems for preserving core values through evolution: Mechanisms that safeguard foundational beliefs even while adjusting how they're lived.

4. Design processes for stakeholder engagement in evolution: Ways to involve people in shaping change, not just reacting to it.

5. Establish measurement systems for evolution success: Metrics and indicators to track the impact and effectiveness of cultural transition.

6. Create communication frameworks for managing change: Narrative and message tools that carry clarity, honesty, and hope.

Deliverables:

- **Evolution Monitoring System:** Scanning tools and pulse checks for timely insight into misalignment or opportunity.

- **Change Management Framework:** Planning templates and tracking tools that guide execution.

- **Core Value Preservation Guidelines:** Distinguishing what is sacred from what is adaptable.

- **Stakeholder Engagement Playbook:** Steps and tactics to involve key voices throughout.

- **Measurement System Documentation:** Balanced use of data, story, and signal to track cultural transition.

- **Communication Strategy Templates:** Ready-to-use guides and messaging tools for use across levels and locations.

Estimated Time: 8–10 weeks

Final Thoughts: Making Culture Your Competitive Advantage

As we've seen throughout Chapters 3 and 4, creating and maintaining a strong culture requires both clear understanding and systematic implementation. The journey from cultural aspiration to cultural excellence demands unwavering commitment, consistent execution, and continuous evolution. Organizations that successfully navigate this journey create sustainable competitive advantages that drive long-term success.

Strong Culture: Implementation Timeline

Month 1–3: Foundation Setting

- **Week 1–2:** Initial stakeholder assessment and engagement planning
- **Week 3–4:** Leadership alignment sessions and commitment building
- **Week 5–8:** Vision, mission, and values development
- **Week 9–12:** Cultural positioning and framework development

Dependencies: Leadership commitment must precede vision development; stakeholder input needed before finalizing cultural positioning

Month 4–6: Infrastructure Building

- **Week 13–16:** System and process alignment
- **Week 17–20:** Ritual and tradition development
- **Week 21–24:** Resource allocation framework creation

Dependencies: Vision and values must be established before system alignment; cultural positioning guides ritual development

Month 7–9: Implementation and Training

- **Week 25–28:** Leadership development program rollout
- **Week 29–32:** Employee training and engagement programs
- **Week 33–36:** Recognition and reinforcement system implementation

Dependencies: Systems and processes must be aligned before training; rituals should be established before recognition systems

Month 10–12: Measurement and Refinement

- **Week 37–40:** Measurement system implementation
- **Week 41–44:** Initial assessment and adjustment
- **Week 45–48:** Refinement of processes and systems

Dependencies: Training must be substantially complete before assessment; measurement systems needed before refinement

Month 13–18: Scaling and Evolution

- **Week 49–56:** Expansion to additional locations/units
- **Week 57–64:** Evolution system implementation
- **Week 65–72:** Long-term sustainability framework development

Dependencies: Core systems must be stable before expansion; measurement systems needed for evolution

Detailed Action Plan for Cultural Implementation

Phase One: Immediate Actions (First 30 Days)

1. **Leadership Preparation**

- Conduct executive team cultural assessment
- Establish cultural steering committee
- Define clear decision rights and responsibilities
- Create communication frameworks

2. **Stakeholder Engagement**

- Map all stakeholder groups and influences
- Develop engagement strategies for each group
- Create feedback collection mechanisms
- Establish communication channels

3. **Resource Allocation**

- Assess current resource distribution
- Identify critical investment needs
- Create cultural investment budget
- Establish tracking mechanisms

Phase Two: Short-Term Focus (31–90 Days)

1. **System Development**

   - Design cultural training programs
   - Create measurement frameworks
   - Develop recognition systems
   - Establish feedback mechanisms

2. **Process Implementation**

   - Roll out initial training modules
   - Implement basic measurement systems
   - Begin recognition programs
   - Start feedback collection

3. **Leadership Engagement**

   - Conduct leadership training
   - Establish accountability systems
   - Create modeling frameworks
   - Begin regular culture discussions

Phase Three: Medium-Term Actions (91–180 Days)

1. **Cultural Reinforcement**

   - Implement full training program
   - Establish regular cultural events
   - Create storytelling frameworks
   - Develop celebration systems

2. **Measurement and Adjustment**

   - Conduct first full assessment
   - Make system adjustments
   - Refine processes
   - Update frameworks as needed

3. **Scaling Preparation**

   - Develop scaling frameworks
   - Create expansion playbooks
   - Establish integration processes
   - Build adaptation guidelines

Phase Four: Long-Term Implementation (181–365 Days)

1. **Evolution Management**

    - Implement evolution sensing systems
    - Create change management frameworks
    - Establish adaptation processes
    - Develop long-term monitoring

2. **Sustainability Development**

    - Create sustainability frameworks
    - Establish ongoing programs
    - Develop future planning processes
    - Build long-term measurement systems

3. **Continuous Improvement**

    - Implement refinement processes
    - Create innovation frameworks
    - Establish review systems
    - Develop enhancement mechanisms

Monitoring Cultural Success: Metrics That Matter

Measuring culture is not about perfection, it's about direction. It's about knowing whether the culture you're building is taking root, how it's showing up, and what needs reinforcement. These checkpoints and metrics are meant to help your organization move from intention to evidence—from ideas to impact.

30-Day Review: Foundation Laid or Just Announced?

Within the first month, the goal is to ensure structural readiness and signal cultural priority.

Foundational Readiness Metrics

- 90% or more of the leadership team engaged in at least one core cultural initiative
- 100% of identified stakeholder groups mapped with corresponding engagement strategies
- Budget allocation explicitly aligned with cultural priorities in operational planning
- Communication channels established with all key stakeholder groups
- Cultural baseline assessment completed with at least 80% employee participation

Cultural Behavior Checkpoints

- 85% of documented leadership decisions reflect awareness of new cultural values
- Initial feedback shows 70% of employees can articulate the organization's cultural intent
- 60% of teams show early signs of adopting one or more key cultural behaviors
- 75% of major decisions include visible cultural considerations
- Resistance patterns identified and addressed in 80% of known cases

90-Day Milestone: Are Systems Reinforcing the Story?

By this stage, the systems that carry and reinforce culture—training, recognition, communication—should be functional and in motion.

Implementation & System Metrics

- Cultural training launched with 85% completion of core modules
- Recognition systems used actively by at least 75% of people leaders
- 70% of employees regularly engaging feedback mechanisms (pulse checks, reflections, etc.)
- 90% of organizational units generating measurable cultural data
- At least 80% of teams participating in newly established cultural rituals or rhythms
- Behavioral Integration Signals
- 75% of employees demonstrate understanding of core values and desired behaviors
- Leadership alignment with cultural values evident in 90% of documented decisions
- 70% of internal communications reflect new cultural language
- Recognition consistently distributed across 85% of departments
- Cultural values showing up in at least 85% of routine, non-symbolic decision-making moments

180-Day Assessment: Integration Becomes Reality

At this point, culture should no longer feel like a pilot—it should be embedded.

Cultural Integration Benchmarks

- 85% of operational decisions reflect stated cultural values
- Employee engagement or alignment scores improve by 20%
- 80% participation rate in recognition programs
- Training completion rates sustained at 90% or higher across all levels
- Feedback loops engaging 80% of the employee population

Operational Alignment Metrics

- 100% of performance reviews include cultural alignment as a criterion
- 90% of budget and resource decisions aligned with cultural goals
- 85% of project plans include cultural considerations
- 75% of customer feedback aligns with core values or service philosophy
- 80% of innovation and change initiatives explicitly grounded in cultural values

365-Day Evaluation: Has Culture Become Identity?

After a year, culture should no longer be a project. It should be who you are.

Cultural Strength Indicators

- 90% of employees report cultural clarity and alignment
- 95% of leadership decisions demonstrate cultural consistency
- 90% of external partnerships and alliances reflect your cultural values
- 85% sustained participation in recognition programs
- 95% training completion for cultural and values-based programs

Business Impact Indicators

- 25% improvement in retention for culturally aligned employees
- 20% rise in customer satisfaction in culture-touchpoint areas
- 30% increase in innovation performance in teams aligned with cultural behaviors
- 15% boost in operational efficiency through cultural alignment
- 10% increase in financial performance in culturally-driven initiatives

Long-Term Sustainability: Can Culture Scale and Evolve?

Strong cultures flex without breaking. They evolve without losing identity.

Scalability & Sustainability Metrics

- Cultural evolution frameworks active in 90% of departments or units
- New initiatives reflect culture in 85% of cases
- 80% of adaptation efforts (acquisitions, expansions, pivots) show effective cultural alignment
- 90% of integration efforts rated successful by stakeholder review
- 85% of teams actively using continuous cultural improvement mechanisms

Qualitative Culture Checkpoints

Numbers tell part of the story. The rest is told in how people feel, speak, and show up.

Leaders should assess qualitative indicators such as:

- How deeply and authentically cultural stories are being shared
- The presence and quality of culture-focused conversations in meetings
- The natural emergence of informal cultural ambassadors
- Whether employees spontaneously reinforce values without being asked
- How often cultural language shows up in hallway and Zoom conversations
- How the workspace visually reflects cultural values
- Whether new practices emerge from teams rather than just from HR

These metrics, both quantitative and qualitative, should be reviewed in light of your organization's position on the cultural strength spectrum (see Chapter 3). Strong cultures don't aim for perfect scores. They aim for consistency, courage, and clarity.

Regular assessment of these checkpoints helps organizations:

1. Identify where energy and resources need to be redirected
2. Celebrate real cultural wins, not performative ones
3. Adjust strategies before cultural drift sets in
4. Keep momentum visible and meaningful
5. Show the ROI of building culture like you mean it

Critical Success Factors for Staying the Course

1. Leadership models cultural values in behavior, not just language
2. Resources flow in alignment with stated cultural commitments
3. Communication stays consistent, honest, and clear
4. Data systems provide real insight—not vanity metrics

Closing Summary: Making Culture a Competitive Advantage

Creating and sustaining a strong, intentional culture is one of the most complex and rewarding commitments an organization can make. As you've seen throughout this chapter, culture doesn't happen by default. It is designed, cultivated, and reinforced—again and again.

In Phase One, we built the cultural foundation—vision, values, mission, and clarity on where you stand. Leaders who do this well don't just name the culture, they make it visible and operational.

Phase Two addressed the infrastructure. Rituals, routines, and shared language become the scaffolding. Resources either affirm or erode culture. Investment must match intention.

In Phase Three, we examined how to reinforce and evolve culture through systems, decision-making, and performance management. Culture is kept alive in everyday choices, not just big events.

Phase Four then turned our focus to scale. Strong cultures must adapt without diluting. That means anchoring identity while creating enough space for local flavor, growth, and innovation.

And now—with the right metrics in hand, and a leadership team willing to live the values daily—you're not just talking culture. You're building one that lasts.

Leadership is the difference. Culture doesn't fail from lack of planning. It fails from lack of ownership. The most compelling culture work happens when leaders stop outsourcing values to HR and start treating culture like the strategic priority it is.

When done with intentionality, culture becomes your sharpest edge in a noisy, distracted world. A culture that speaks through action. A culture that draws the right people in and repels the wrong ones out. A culture that scales, evolves, and endures.

And that's how you make culture your advantage. Not your campaign.

Let it live. Let it lead. Let it last.

CHAPTER 5

IGNITING ORGANIZATIONAL HEARTBEAT ENGAGEMENT
DISCRETIONARY EFFORT, LOYALTY, AND ADVOCACY

Up to this point, we've talked a lot about what makes a strong culture—clarity, consistency, intentionality—without weighing in too heavily on what values an organization should choose. We've been value-agnostic by design. Why? Because what makes a culture strong isn't its slogans. It's whether people inside the system actually live what the organization claims to believe. Culture, as we've seen, is not about being nice, it's about being clear.

A strong culture sharpens decision-making. When your values are visible and behaviorally embedded, you don't need a committee for every choice. People know what to do because they understand the ground they're standing on. That kind of cultural clarity also streamlines collaboration. Teams move faster. Less politicking. Less second-guessing. More flow.

It gets even better. That same clarity acts like a magnetic field. It draws in people who say "yes, this feels like me," and it repels those who won't thrive in that ecosystem. Hiring gets tighter. Onboarding gets shorter. Accountability becomes obvious. When everyone knows what's expected, slippage doesn't go unnoticed, it stands out. And it doesn't have to be punished; it's just not sustainable.

But let's zoom in even further. The real win of a strong culture isn't just organizational alignment. its emotional activation. People stop working for you and start working with you. They start bringing parts of themselves that were previously dormant—ideas, passion, grit. Culture, when it's lived, makes work personal in the best way. People care more. They try harder. And they don't need to be chased to do it.

Here's the point: none of this is about which values you choose. It's about how consistently and honestly you practice them. That's what creates emotional engagement. And emotional engagement is what unlocks the three forces we're going to focus on now—discretionary effort, loyalty, and advocacy.

These aren't just buzzwords or feel-good HR goals. They're strategic drivers. When these elements are alive in your organization, you don't have to manufacture motivation. It's already built in.

Let's unpack each one.

Discretionary Effort

This is the bonus fuel. The above-and-beyond energy people give when no one is watching. You can't pay for it. You can't require it. You can't legislate it into existence. Marcus Buckingham explains it beautifully, it only shows up when people feel seen for their strengths, aligned with their role, and confident that what they bring matters.

It's the difference between someone who does their job and someone who owns it. Between a clock-puncher and a culture carrier.

Loyalty

Not the kind that shows up on a tenure report. Loyalty is emotional, not procedural. It's when someone stays not because they have to, but because they want to. It shows up when they defend the organization in rooms you're not in. When they choose you again and again, even when other offers come in.

This kind of loyalty is rare. And it's only built through trust, connection, and the unshakable belief that the organization has meaning.

Advocacy

Advocacy is the echo of culture. It's when people talk about you the way you want to be known. It's Glassdoor reviews you didn't write, Instagram stories from employees without a PR team, volunteers who bring friends not because they're asked—but because they believe. Advocacy is a powerful cultural indicator. It tells you whether people feel proud of what they're part of. And pride doesn't come from perks. It comes from purpose.

Together, these three elements—discretionary effort, loyalty, and advocacy—form the heartbeat of an engaged, high-impact organization. They are how culture moves from aspiration to activation. So yes, strong cultures can drive these outcomes. But let's not be naïve. They can also kill them—if poorly built, rigidly policed, or self-serving in their design.

Let's start with the bright side.

How a Strong Culture Can Induce Engagement

Igniting Discretionary Effort: Going Above and Beyond

Alignment with Purpose:

I once worked with a CHRO who said, "People give more when they believe more." She wasn't talking about bonuses. She was talking about meaning.

Imagine a workplace where everyone, from entry-level to executive, sees their work as tied to something bigger than themselves. When people believe they're building something that matters, energy multiplies. They don't wait to be asked—they offer. They innovate. They stretch.

That's what cultural alignment does. It doesn't just tell people what the organization stands for. It makes them feel it—and act accordingly.

Recognition of Strengths:

When culture is strong, people don't feel invisible. They feel known. And they don't have to be loud to be seen. One CEO I worked with revamped his recognition program to highlight effort, not just outcomes. The result? People started leaning in—taking more initiative, contributing in new ways—because they knew their uniqueness was valued, not buried under a role description.

When leaders recognize and reward individual strengths—when they say, "you bring something vital here"—discretionary effort becomes the norm, not the exception.

Building Loyalty: A Culture Worth Defending

Emotional Connection:

Loyalty is rooted in belonging. And belonging isn't built with swag or slogans. It's built when people look around and say, "These are my people."
When culture reflects the values and aspirations of the people within it, emotional bonds form. Employees don't just comply—they commit. They defend the culture. They stay through turbulence. Because it's not just work. It's theirs.

Consistency and Trust:

Loyalty shrivels in the face of inconsistency. If your stated values say one thing and your leaders do another, don't expect people to stay loyal—they'll stay cautious.

Trust grows when culture is practiced predictably. When values aren't just wall art but operating principles. When feedback isn't weaponized, and accountability isn't one-sided.

In environments like this, people believe the organization has integrity. And they return the favor—with their trust, and with their tenure.

Turning Members into Promoters: Advocacy and Evangelism

Pride and Ownership:

People talk about what they're proud of. If they're not talking about your organization, that might be the real engagement metric you need to worry about.

When culture works, advocacy isn't a campaign, it's a reflex. People share wins, invite others in, and represent the organization like it's part of their own identity. They feel pride not because it's perfect, but because it's theirs.

Collective Identity:

The best advocacy comes from alignment with a shared identity. When people don't just work at an organization but identify with it, their voice carries more weight.

They speak as insiders, as believers, as witnesses to what it's really like inside the culture. And that advocacy lands with authenticity. Because it isn't paid for. It's lived.

Of course, culture has a dark side when misdirected. A strong culture that forgets why it exists, or excludes those who think differently, can crush the very engagement it hopes to inspire.

But when done right—when it's rooted in purpose, practiced with integrity, and built to include rather than exclude, strong culture does more than create alignment.

It ignites a heartbeat.

Challenging Discretionary Effort

Stifled Innovation

In environments where norms and expectations are fixed, the freedom to experiment and innovate can quickly diminish. Employees may feel that established boundaries are sacrosanct, which discourages them from proposing new ideas or taking creative risks. As Buckingham and Coffman argue in First, Break All the Rules (1999), when individuals perceive little room to deviate from the norm, the extra creativity that defines true discretionary effort is suppressed. Edgar Schein (2010) similarly notes that overly rigid cultural expectations can curtail innovation, leaving little space for breakthrough ideas.

Instruction for Leaders:

Audit the spoken and unspoken "rules of engagement" in your culture. Are there invisible guardrails that make deviation feel unsafe? Encourage team members to share when they've felt blocked from suggesting or trying something new. Then remove those friction points publicly, signaling that innovation is worth the risk.

Reduced Autonomy

An intense focus on "the way things are done" often creates a climate where deviation is not tolerated. When individuals worry that any departure from standard practices will be met with disapproval, they are less likely to invest the extra energy that characterizes discretionary effort. Schein (2010) highlights that excessive standardization can erode personal autonomy, leading to a situation where employees and members become risk averse, even when novel approaches might benefit the organization.

Instruction for Leaders:

Revisit standard operating procedures, especially where there's high employee turnover or burnout. Ask managers to identify one area where autonomy could be increased and monitor whether engagement or performance improves in that space.

Lack of Personalized Contribution

A strong culture that enforces a one-size-fits-all approach may inadvertently marginalize unique strengths. As Deal and Kennedy (1982) explain in Corporate Cultures, when contributions do not fit the prescribed mold, they risk being overlooked or undervalued. This lack of recognition can cause capable individuals to withhold extra effort, as their distinctive talents are not seen as integral to the organization's success.

Instruction for Leaders:

Make recognition personal. Move beyond standardized employee awards. Train managers to identify and appreciate unique talents—even when they don't fit the dominant mold. Create space in team meetings for people to share passion projects or lesser-known skill sets.

Shaking Loyalty

Forced Conformity

When loyalty is measured by strict adherence to rigid cultural norms, individuals may feel compelled to remain with an organization out of obligation rather than genuine commitment. Buckingham and Coffman (1999) emphasize that authentic loyalty arises from emotional engagement rather than mere conformity. When the pressure to conform overshadows personal values, loyalty becomes brittle and superficial, lacking the resilience of true commitment.

Instruction for Leaders:

Don't confuse compliance with commitment. Include values-alignment questions in stay interviews, pulse surveys, and exit interviews. If people are staying but feeling suffocated, your culture is breeding silent resentment, not loyalty.

Exclusion of Diverse Perspectives

An overly homogeneous culture that rewards only those who fit a narrow set of expectations can alienate individuals who might otherwise enrich the organization with fresh insights. Deal and Kennedy (1982) warn that such a culture limits the variety of perspectives that contribute to meaningful progress. By sidelining diversity, the organization risks diminishing the depth and authenticity of loyalty among its broader membership.

Instruction for Leaders:

Audit who gets promoted. Who's in the "inner circle"? Who gets second chances? If everyone looks the same, went to the same schools, or thinks the same way, you're not building loyalty, you're cloning dependence.

Superficial Attachment

The pressure to adhere to a rigid cultural framework can result in a façade of loyalty—where outward expressions of commitment mask an inner disconnect. As observed by Buckingham and Coffman (1999), this superficial attachment fails to foster the deep emotional bonds necessary for enduring loyalty. When employees or members feel coerced into conformity, the resulting loyalty is more about external expectations than internal conviction.

Instruction for Leaders:

Ask yourself: When's the last time someone challenged leadership—without consequences? Superficial loyalty looks good on a dashboard but disappears in crisis. Create channels for real, even unpopular, feedback.

Risking Advocacy

Inauthentic Endorsement

Advocacy should stem from a genuine belief in the organization's mission, but when culture pressures individuals to speak positively regardless of their true feelings, endorsements can feel insincere. Forced advocacy, as noted by Buckingham and Coffman (1999), can backfire if stakeholders sense that the support is not heartfelt. This inauthenticity undermines the credibility of the organization's message.

Instruction for Leaders:

Listen to how people talk about your organization when they think you're not listening. Real advocacy sounds unscripted. Equip brand ambassadors with your story, then empower them to share it in their own voice—not a corporate echo.

Risk of Groupthink

A culture that discourages dissent fosters an environment where advocacy is based on a single, unchallenged narrative. Irving Janis (1972) discusses how groupthink can suppress diverse viewpoints, leading to a narrow and uncritical form of advocacy. Without constructive debate, the organization loses the benefits of varied insights, reducing its ability to evolve and improve its practices. Such disadvantages are often seen in organizations that practice nepotistic hiring and recruitment.

Instruction for Leaders:

If no one's playing devil's advocate, you're not innovating. Rotate responsibility in meetings for raising the contrarian view. Protect people who speak truth to power—publicly.

Dangers of Nepotism

Nepotism and cronyism can be very dangerous to organizational excellence. Typically, when organizations have a pattern of nepotism in their recruitment, accountability and performance are compromised (Catmull and Wallace, 2014). Individuals enter the organization with an instant rank that is often not based upon merit, but relationship favor. Such nepotism can inhibit creativity and risk-taking, given the limited thought style that comes with leaders hiring people just like them. Homogeneity reinforces what already exists in the organization while limiting its growth.

Similarly, Khurana (2007) views nepotism as a cultural impediment. It discourages dissent that could otherwise bring about faster problem-solving, better practices, and intellectual growth.

Instruction for Leaders:

If you're tempted to hire someone "you know," be honest—do they stretch your organization or reflect it? If they only reflect it, you're multiplying your blind spots.

Limited External Appeal

When advocacy is built solely on internal conformity, it may fail to resonate with a broader audience. Genuine advocacy requires a dynamic interplay of personal conviction and diverse perspectives—qualities that a rigid culture may not support. As Deal and Kennedy (1982) argue, an insular cultural focus can make the organization's message seem narrow and unrelatable, diminishing its potential to build widespread external support.

Instruction for Leaders:

Test your story with outsiders. Does your mission land the same with partners, customers, and recruits? If it doesn't translate beyond your walls, you're preaching to a choir that's shrinking.

A Strong Culture: To Be or Not to Be?

At this point, you may be wondering—is a strong culture still worth it? I would argue yes. The purpose of a strong culture is not to oppress individuals but to unite them around values and behaviors that align with the organization's goals. A strong culture does not mean a homogeneous organization. It means homogeneity in values and behaviors that fuel the mission.

A strong organizational culture, as argued by Schein (2010) and Buckingham and Coffman (1999), is a unifying framework that aligns diverse individuals around a common cause. It is not about sameness. It is about shared purpose.

Uniting Through Shared Values, Not Uniformity

A strong culture is fundamentally about creating common ground. This alignment allows people from all walks of life to work toward the same objectives. It becomes a compass, not a cage. Schein (2010) emphasizes that such alignment provides a platform for risk-taking and innovation, not just predictability and compliance.

Example: Pixar's Culture of Creativity

Pixar's strong culture is not based on conformity but on shared creative purpose. As Catmull and Wallace detail in Creativity, Inc. (2014), the company fosters innovation by anchoring its employees to a clear mission while creating room for uniqueness and experimentation. That's the sweet spot leaders must aim for: shared standards, personal freedom.

Distinction Between Homogeneity and Alignment

A strong culture aligns people. It does not assimilate them. You don't need everyone to think the same, you need everyone to move in the same direction. When that happens, creative conflict becomes constructive. Without that alignment, even the best ideas get drowned in a sea of misalignment and political silos.

The Benefits of Diversity Within a Strong Culture

Diversity, when it exists inside a strong cultural frame, is rocket fuel. Page (2007) shows that diverse teams outperform homogenous ones in solving complex problems. But only if there's a shared platform of trust and purpose. Culture is that platform.

What This Means for You

If you are a CEO, pastor, CHRO, or civic leader, don't throw out your strong culture because you fear rigidity. Refine it. Reclaim it. Redefine it as the mechanism that aligns unique individuals around your highest vision. Culture isn't your enemy. Unconscious culture is.

Now that we've explored how strong cultures can either protect or undermine discretionary effort, loyalty, and advocacy, it's time to explore the core components that make engagement sustainable. Not surface-level buy-in. Deep, consistent, purpose-fueled engagement. Let's go there.

CASE STUDIES
LESSONS FROM STRONG CULTURES

Culture is a flexible tool and mechanism. It is used as the carrot and/or the stick, the weapon or the helping hand. While culture is everything, sometimes its seems as if it's nothing at all. Culture is the best kept secret that is finally getting out. Leaders in the corporate, civic, nonprofit and religious worlds alike, finally realize the power in using culture. The greatest leaders and organizations are recognizing the power in creating culture, intentionally.

What is so powerful about culture is that it can be an influential, moving and impactful force in any type of organization. In this segment of the book, we are going to dive deep into a variety of organizations. What the case studies will reveal is that organizations with contrasting values, regardless of sector, can be successful. Success is defined by achieving their organizational goals at the level desired or above.

What these organizations have in common is that they have very strong cultures. Again, strong is defined as a culture that is very specific in defining their shared values, beliefs, norms and practices of their organization AND behave with strong adherence to their stated shared values, beliefs, norms and stated practices with great consistency. To illustrate this point, we will examine organizations with contrasting values in multiple sectors. What we will identify is the level of success that all the organizations are able to attain in spite of their contrasting cultures. We will discuss how their strong cultures have helped them to excel.

Some of the world's strongest cultures exist in environments where the stakes are highest and the bonds are deepest—military units like the Navy SEALs and U.S. Marine Corps or tightly knit communities such as fraternities and sororities. These institutions build cultures that are unmistakably strong, often producing lifelong loyalty, unwavering adherence to shared norms, and a powerful sense of belonging.

What drives this level of cultural strength?

It is rarely accidental. These environments are built on the foundation of:

- **Forced shared experiences,** often traumatic or intensely challenging
- **Rituals and rites of passage,** sometimes formal, sometimes informal
- **Clear identity and symbolism,** reflected in language, attire, and behavior
- **Exclusive belonging,** where entry is earned and commitment is expected

In the military, recruits are tested physically and mentally through structured boot camps and deployments that forge identity through endurance. In Greek life, social bonds are cemented through shared initiation rites, loyalty to traditions, and a deep sense of group identity that often lasts for decades.

These conditions create cultural clarity and behavioral consistency, which align closely with the definition of strong culture we have been using, specificity in shared values, beliefs, norms, and practices, paired with consistent adherence across the organization.

However, most companies do not, and cannot, replicate these high-intensity conditions. Trauma is not a sustainable or ethical tool for culture-building in business. Exclusivity and forced cohesion can backfire in environments that require inclusion, psychological safety, and diverse collaboration.

Still, there is something to be learned from these models. The commitment, the clarity, the rituals, the pride—all can be thoughtfully translated into corporate environments, minus the extremity. The organizations we explore in this chapter demonstrate how it is possible to build strong, distinctive cultures in the real world of business—without boot camps or battlefields.

What follows is a look at companies from vastly different sectors and belief systems—Virgin, Siemens, Chick-fil-A, and Al Rajhi Bank, each with its own take on strong culture. From radical freedom to disciplined faith, they offer valuable insights into how intentional culture, when aligned and consistently practiced, becomes a strategic advantage. This chapter explores what they do, how they do it, and why their success isn't rooted in what they believe, but in how strongly they believe it and how consistently they live it.

Siemens vs. Virgin: Precision vs. Play — Two Strong Cultures, Two Very Different Worlds

Let us begin with two giants that could not feel more different. One born in 19th-century Germany, the other launched in the rebellious spirit of 1970s Britain. One builds turbines, railways, and medical imaging equipment. The other builds airlines, music labels, and experiences that stretch from earth to outer space. One thrives on compliance, structure, and engineering rigor. The other thrives on creativity, irreverence, and calculated risk. At face value, Siemens and Virgin are cultural opposites. Yet beneath the contrast lies a fascinating truth — both organizations are built on remarkably strong cultures.

And not just strong in a general sense. Strong as defined in this book — a culture that clearly articulates its shared values, beliefs, norms, and practices and lives them out with extraordinary consistency. These are companies that know exactly who they are and behave like it, not occasionally, but always. That is the key.

Strong culture is not about style, it is about substance. It is not about being loud or quiet, formal or fun, but about being aligned and intentional. Siemens and Virgin show us that strong culture is not a one-size-fits-all formula. It is a custom suit tailored to the company's identity, goals, and way of being. Let us start with Siemens.

Siemens: Structure as a Strategic Advantage

Founded in 1847, Siemens has grown into one of the world's most respected industrial manufacturing and technology companies. With operations in over 190 countries and a workforce of more than 300,000 people, Siemens has mastered the art of complexity. What allows it to function effectively at such scale is not just operational excellence, it is cultural clarity.

Siemens is the embodiment of German engineering values. It is precise, rational, disciplined, and reliable. These are not just adjectives, they are operating principles. At Siemens, structure is not red tape, it is a roadmap. Hierarchy is not a hindrance; it is a way to honor expertise and ensure accountability. Compliance is not a constraint; it is a commitment to excellence and safety.

The culture at Siemens is formal but not cold. It is hierarchical but still meritocratic. It is process-driven but still innovative. Innovation at Siemens does not look like rapid brainstorming or agile sprints. It looks like carefully funded R&D projects, meticulous testing, and technologies that can support infrastructure and lives across decades. It is innovation with a long-term horizon, guided by discipline rather than urgency.

Siemens is a culture of mastery. Employees are expected to be experts, not just in their roles, but in their responsibility to uphold the integrity of the organization. There is pride in precision, in getting it right, in building things that endure. This is what makes Siemens a trusted name across the globe. From high-speed trains to MRI machines, Siemens delivers because its culture demands it.

And that culture is lived, not laminated. Leaders model it. Systems reinforce it. Employees internalize it. The result is not just high performance, but high consistency. That is the signature of a strong culture. Now let us turn to Virgin.

Virgin: Culture as Brand, Brand as Culture

If Siemens is a carefully composed symphony, Virgin is a high-energy jam session. It is bold, improvisational, and unmistakably human. Founded by Richard Branson in 1970, Virgin has launched more than 400 companies and built a brand that is as iconic as it is elastic. Virgin has touched everything from music to aviation to mobile to space. But the secret to its cohesion is not found in strategy decks, it is found in culture.

Virgin's culture is irreverent, fun, and fiercely people centered. It thrives on a challenging spirit, a desire to disrupt industries not just for the sake of profit, but to make them more enjoyable, more ethical, and more customer-friendly. That purpose is not vague, it is lived. It shows up in product design, customer service, and the tone of every brand touchpoint.

At Virgin, the values are not words on a wall, they are the personality of the place. Employees are encouraged to be themselves. Risk is celebrated. Mistakes are treated as part of the process. The culture is built on trust, freedom, and creativity. Flat structures support open communication. Autonomy fuels innovation. And fun is not an afterthought — it is a strategic choice.
Where Siemens values mastery, Virgin values momentum. Where Siemens honors tradition, Virgin honors reinvention. But like Siemens, Virgin is consistent. It does not betray its identity to chase trends. It does not abandon its values to appease investors. It leans into what makes it unique — and scales it.

Richard Branson is not just a founder. He is a culture carrier. His personal values are embedded into the DNA of the organization. His leadership is relational, experiential, and deeply human. He does not manage Virgin from a distance. He lives it. And that presence reinforces the culture in powerful ways.

Virgin's success is not the result of luck or marketing genius. It is the result of cultural intentionality. The brand works because the culture is real. The experience feels cohesive because the values are practiced. And people come back — as employees, as customers, and as fans — because they know exactly what Virgin stands for.

Two Roads, One Destination

So what do Siemens and Virgin have in common? They are both extremely successful. They both operate globally. They both innovate in their own ways. But more importantly, they both have strong cultures. Cultures that are defined, lived, and reinforced at every level of the organization.

Their values could not be more different. Their industries are worlds apart. Their internal dynamics contrast sharply. Yet both companies thrive. Why? Because they are clear about who they are and consistent in how they operate. That is the secret.

Strong culture is not about being the same. It is about being specific and then being steadfast.

Siemens wins through precision. Virgin wins through personality. Siemens builds systems. Virgin builds excitement. Siemens scales through rigor. Virgin scales through resonance. Both cultures work because they are congruent with their mission, their leadership, and their day-to-day behavior.

What this case study reveals is something powerful: You do not need to copy anyone else's culture to be successful. You just need to build one that is authentic and then live it with discipline. Whether you are running a legacy infrastructure company or launching a brand into orbit, culture can be your greatest differentiator — not because it looks a certain way, but because it feels the same, everywhere, every time.
Siemens and Virgin prove that culture is not about conformity. It is about clarity. And when clarity meets consistency, you get the kind of culture that does not just attract people — it keeps them, inspires them, and turns them into ambassadors of something meaningful.

That is the power of a strong culture. And that is why culture, when done right, is not soft. It is strategic.

Siemens vs. Virgin Group

CHARACTERISTICS	SIEMENS (FORMAL & STRUCTURED)	VIRGIN GROUP (FUN & ADVENTUROUS)
Employee Value Proposition	Offers stability, career longevity, and global expertise	Offers creative freedom, individuality, and a high-energy culture
Industry Strength	Global leader in industrial automation, smart infrastructure, Medtech, and energy	Bold multi-sector disruptor in travel, telecom, space, and leisure
Revenue & Scale	Over $84 billion USD annually with operations in 190+ countries	Estimated $20-25 billion USD across 40+ brand ventures
Innovation Approach	Invests billions in structured R&D for engineering, automation, and sustainability	Thrives on market disruption and bold ideas (Virgin Galactic, Virgin Voyages)
Business Model	Centralized, high-compliance, B2B-heavy contracts and infrastructure deals	Decentralized, brand licensing model focused on consumer experience
Reputation	Known for precision, reliability, and engineering excellence	Known for bold branding, customer experience, and risk-taking
Leadership Brand	CEO-led, traditional corporate governance	Founder-branded success story (Richard Branson = brand magnet)
Global Impact	Shapes future of mobility, health tech, and climate tech	Elevates lifestyle and accessibility in industries like air travel and finance
Resilience & Longevity	Founded in 1847, has weathered wars, digital transitions, and global economic shifts	Reinvented itself multiple times since 1970, scaling across diverse sectors
Cultural Fit	Ideal for engineers, strategists, and policy-focused innovators	Ideal for creatives, risk-takers, and visionary entrepreneurs

Amazon vs. Google: Productivity vs. Humanity — Two Paths to Business Greatness

If Siemens and Virgin are opposites on a scale of structure and spirit, then Amazon and Google are a collision of different kinds of brilliance. One is obsessed with speed, precision, and domination. The other is obsessed with ideas, possibility, and people. One wants to deliver your package in under 24 hours. The other wants to map your brain, predict your next thought, and invent the future.

This is not just a battle between two tech giants. It is a contrast between two deep cultural philosophies, one driven by productivity at scale, the other shaped by humanity-centered innovation.

But here is the twist. Like Siemens and Virgin, both companies are highly successful. Both are cultural powerhouses. And both live their values with consistency and conviction, which is what qualifies them as having strong cultures. Let us begin with Amazon.

Amazon: Culture as a High-Performance Machine

Amazon is not just a company. It is a system, engineered for efficiency, speed, and domination. With $574.8 billion in annual revenue, it is the largest of all the companies profiled in this chapter. Its power lies in its ability to do more, faster, and at larger scale than almost any other company in history. Its culture reflects that.

Amazon is often described as intense. Fast. Unforgiving. It is a place where performance is everything. Innovation is measured in hours, not months. Employees are pushed, stretched, and sometimes burned out. But here is the key: it works for the people who choose it.

Amazon's culture is rooted in a productivity ethos. It hires ambitious, often type-A individuals who want to be challenged. The company's infamous leadership principles are not window dressing, they are how performance is assessed, promotions are earned, and decisions are made. These principles, like "Customer Obsession," "Deliver Results," and "Insist on the Highest Standards," form a behavioral contract. Everyone knows the expectations.

The culture is not for everyone, and Amazon does not pretend otherwise. In fact, part of the company's strength is in that very clarity. You either thrive in that environment, or you opt out. And that is by design.

Employees are offered generous severance packages if they feel the company is not a fit. This keeps cultural alignment high. The result? Amazon may have high churn, but it attracts and retains people who match the pace. This is strong culture by the book: specific values, clearly communicated, and lived out in consistent ways.

Amazon's innovation approach is not focused on moonshots. It focuses on systems, logistics, and process scale. Whether through the same-day delivery, Alexa voice services, or AWS cloud infrastructure, the company invents with operational excellence in mind. It is less about imagination, more about implementation.

Jeff Bezos once said, "We are willing to be misunderstood for long periods of time." That sentiment underpins Amazon's unflinching confidence in its model, even when critics question its labor practices or management style. The company is unapologetic about what it is, and that is part of its cultural strength. Let us now contrast that with Google.

Google: Culture as a Canvas for Possibility

Where Amazon thrives on pressure, Google thrives on possibility. Where Amazon optimizes for efficiency, Google optimizes for ideas. If Amazon is a machine, Google is a laboratory, humming with creativity, experimentation, and human insight.

Google's culture is often associated with bean bags, free food, and smart people solving big problems. But dig deeper, and you find a sophisticated philosophy centered on trust, autonomy, and purposeful invention.

With $323.6 billion in annual revenue, Google (Alphabet) remains a powerhouse, not just in advertising and search, but in shaping how we think, work, and interact with the digital world. But it is how Google creates that impact that makes its culture strong.

Google believes in the long view. Innovation is not just about what can be built fast. It is about what can be imagined deeply. From Google Search to Gmail to Android to the AI labs powering Bard and DeepMind, the company prioritizes depth over speed.

And it hires accordingly. Google is renowned for its ability to attract top global talent. But more importantly, it retains them. It does this by fostering a culture that feels human-centered. Employees are given room to think, question, challenge. Risk is encouraged, but so is psychological safety. That combination is rare, and powerful.

Where Amazon's Employee Value Proposition is challenge and impact, Google's is growth and meaning. It is not that people do not work hard at Google. They do. But they work hard in a context that also prioritizes well-being, inclusivity, and intellectual freedom.

And like Amazon, Google has its own set of cultural anchors. From OKRs to its long-standing mission to "organize the world's information and make it universally accessible and useful," its purpose is more than marketing. It is embedded in the way the company approaches product development, strategy, and even performance reviews.

One of the reasons Google's culture is admired is because it marries visionary ambition with a sincere care for people. You are not just hired to execute. You are hired to imagine, contribute, and stretch the edge of what is possible. That is a very different form of strength.

Two Cultures, Two Engines of Innovation

So here we are again, two giants, two radically different cultures, both thriving.

Amazon measures success in velocity, volume, and scale. Google measures success in impact, insight, and ingenuity. Amazon optimizes for operational dominance. Google optimizes for creative advantage. Amazon believes in discipline. Google believes in discovery.

Yet both share the core of what makes a strong culture: clarity and consistency.

Neither company hides who it is. Neither company dilutes its beliefs to appeal to everyone. Both are unapologetically themselves. And both deliver extraordinary results.

Google is not better than Amazon. Amazon is not better than Google. They are simply different and deeply aligned to who they are.

That is what strong culture is. Not about being right. Not about being best. About being true.

Whether you want to build the fastest delivery system in history or the smartest AI assistant in the world, the lesson is the same: culture is not a custom. It is your operating system. When that system is designed with intention, and practiced with integrity, it does not just produce success, it produces sustainability.

That is the story of Amazon and Google. Two paths. One truth. Culture, when strong, does not have to look the same. It just has to feel the same, to everyone living it.

CHARACTERISTICS	AMAZON (PRODUCTIVITY-FOCUSED)	GOOGLE (HUMANITY-CENTERED INNOVATION)
Employee Value Proposition	High churn but attracts ambitious, driven talent	High retention, attracts top global talent in tech
Annual Revenue (2023)	$574.8 billion	$323.6 billion
Operating Model	Hyper-efficient, logistics-driven, scale at speed	Platform-based, product-focused, innovation at depth
Profit Drivers	AWS (cloud), e-commerce, Prime membership	Advertising (Search + YouTube), Google Cloud, Android
Innovation Output	Iterative, operational (e.g., same-day delivery, Alexa)	Experimental, long-term (e.g., AI, DeepMind, Waymo)
Time-to-Market Speed	Extremely fast–builds, tests, and deploys at scale	Slower but deliberate–deep R&D, user testing
Market Dominance	#1 in global e-commerce & cloud (AWS)	#1 in global search, digital ads, mobile OS (Android)
Talent Acquisition & Retention	High churn but attracts ambitious, driven talent	High retention, attracts top global talent in tech
Customer Loyalty	Amazon Prime: ~200M members globally	Google Search & Gmail: >1B users each; Android on 70%+ phones
Reputation for Innovation	Operational innovation and scale efficiency	Cutting-edge AI, moonshot thinking (e.g., X, Bard, Gemini)
Workplace Awards	Few "Best Place to Work" recognitions due to culture scrutiny	Consistently ranked among top workplaces globally

Samsung vs. IKEA: Prestige vs. Purpose — Two Strong Cultures Shaped by Different North Stars

Some companies build greatness by climbing the mountain of prestige. Others by rooting themselves in purpose. Samsung and IKEA could not be more different in how they define success, shape employee experience, or present themselves to the world, and yet both are unmistakably strong in culture.

Samsung is a global powerhouse driven by ambition, status, and innovation at scale. IKEA is a mission-centered movement wrapped in humble furniture and Scandinavian sensibility. One rises on the back of hierarchy and legacy, the other expands through community and simplicity. But when it comes to cultural clarity and consistency, they both stand tall. Let us begin with Samsung.

Samsung: Power, Precision, and Performance

Samsung is one of South Korea's crown jewels, a company that has become synonymous with national pride and global technological leadership. With over $221 billion in revenue from Samsung Electronics alone, the company operates at a scale few others can rival.
But what fuels this giant? Culture.

Samsung's culture is intense, ambitious, and deeply hierarchical. Its roots in the chaebol system, powerful family-controlled conglomerates, are visible in how decisions flow top-down and influence radiates from the center. The values here are clarity, speed, and results. Success is a product of structure, discipline, and elite performance.

Employees operate in a culture of formality and excellence. The company prizes hierarchy and reward systems that mirror military-like precision. Prestige, innovation, and authority are the cultural currencies. You do not simply show up to work at Samsung. You enter a system designed to mold you, test you, and elevate you, if you can keep up.

It is a place for those who seek high stakes and high achievement. Decisions come from the top, and accountability is sharp. The internal culture often reflects South Korea's broader societal values: respect for elders, loyalty to leadership, and a relentless focus on advancement.

Yet it is not static. Samsung continues to push innovation not only in its products but in its cultural evolution. While hierarchy still reigns, the company is responding to the need for creative agility and global thinking. It is making strides in sustainability and expanding its appeal to younger, more socially conscious talent.

Still, the heart of Samsung's strong culture is unchanged: performance-driven hierarchy, structured decision-making, and relentless pursuit of excellence.

Now let us turn to IKEA.

IKEA: Humility, Humanity, and Home

If Samsung is an empire, IKEA is a village. And that is the point.

Founded in Sweden and now a global retail giant with more than $52.5 billion in annual revenue (Ingka Group), IKEA has built one of the world's most beloved brands by doing the opposite of what most companies do. IKEA's culture is not about power. It is about people.

The organizational structure is famously flat. Everyone is on a first-name basis. Leaders are accessible. Decision-making is collective. And at every level, the values of humility, affordability, and simplicity are celebrated, not just preached.

Workplace culture at IKEA is grounded in co-creation and respect. Employees are not seen as parts of a machine, but as co-workers and contributors. Voices are invited, not managed. Empowerment is practiced, not promised.

This is a company that lives its mission: to create a better everyday life for the many people. That mission is not just about customers — it includes employees. IKEA encourages work-life balance, development at your own pace, and doing work that matters.

Even the cultural symbols reflect this ethos, from do-it-yourself furniture to the flat-pack packaging, from Swedish meatballs to their no-tie dress code, everything says, we are accessible, honest, and equal.

What makes IKEA's culture strong is not flash. It is consistency. The experience inside the company reflects the values portrayed outside. That alignment builds trust. Employees feel part of something bigger than business.

Prestige vs. Purpose, Still Strong

So here we are again. Samsung and IKEA, two companies that seem like cultural opposites. One obsessed with scale, status, and innovation. The other with simplicity, community, and mission.

But they share something powerful: a clearly defined and lived-out culture.

Both are unapologetically themselves. Samsung is for high achievers who crave structure and ambition. IKEA is for team players who value equality and meaning. Neither company tries to be all things to all people. And that is their superpower.

Each company attracts a certain kind of talent, not through perks, but through clarity. Samsung calls to those who want to rise in a performance-driven system. IKEA calls to those who want to grow in a values-driven community.

Cultural strength does not require cultural sameness. It requires identity, intention, and integrity.

Samsung and IKEA prove that whether you lead with hierarchy or humility, what matters is that you lead with alignment. You say who you are. You show who you are. And you stay true to it, not just in boardrooms and slogans, but in policies, practices, and everyday behavior.

That is strong culture. And that is why both Samsung and IKEA succeed, because they do not just have strategy. They have soul.

CHARACTERISTICS	SAMSUNG (HIERARCHICAL, POWER-DRIVEN)	IKEA (FLAT, HUMBLE, EMPLOYEE-DRIVEN)
Employee Value Proposition	High-performance culture offering global exposure, strong hierarchy, and opportunities for rapid advancement tied to achievement. Appeals to those driven by ambition, structure, and technical excellence.	Supportive, inclusive environment that promotes work-life balance, development at your own pace, and contribution to a mission of better everyday living. Appeals to those who value collaboration, authenticity, and purpose.
Organizational Structure	Strongly top-down, status-focused	Flat, non-hierarchical, first-name basis
Leadership Style	Authoritative, legacy-based (chaebol family influence)	Servant-leadership, collective decision-making
Workplace Culture	High-pressure, performance-driven, formal	Collaborative, humble, grounded in equality
Employee Empowerment	Limited; decisions flow from senior leadership	Strong; co-workers encouraged to solve and speak up
Cultural Symbols	Prestige, authority, scale	Simplicity, frugality, accessibility
Global Reputation	Elite tech brand, driven by innovation + power	Value-based global brand, trusted for people-first ethos
Annual Revenue (2023)	~$221 billion USD (Samsung Electronics alone)	~$52.5 billion USD (Ingka Group—main IKEA retail arm)
Time-to-Market Speed	Fast and aggressive—vertically integrated manufacturing	Intentional and consistent—focuses on durability + affordability
Sustainability Strategy	Growing emphasis but still evolving	Strong sustainability mission—circular design, renewable materials
Customer Loyalty	Tech enthusiasts loyal to Galaxy ecosystem and hardware quality	Deep emotional connection due to brand values and affordability

2819 Church vs. Lakewood Church

Culture in the Church: Accountability vs. Affirmation, Two Spiritual Blueprints with One Shared Power

Culture is not confined to the boardroom. It is not limited to corporations or startups or five-year business strategies. Some of the strongest cultures in the world are not found in tech companies or on Wall Street, but in sanctuaries, worship centers, and church pews. And like every other type of organization, churches that thrive long term are the ones that know exactly who they are and behave like it.

Let us look at two churches with incredibly distinct expressions of faith, both wildly successful in their own right: 2819 Church and Lakewood Church. One is obedience-focused, the other grace-focused. One leads with accountability and submission, the other with acceptance and affirmation. But here is the catch, they are both strong cultures. Not because they believe the same thing, but because they embody their beliefs with clarity, consistency, and conviction.

2819 Church: The Culture of Obedience and Sacred Accountability

2819 Church does not soften its message. It does not modernize for palatability. It does not bend toward comfort. The entire structure of the church is built around reverence, holiness, and deep accountability to the Word of God.

This is a spiritual culture where obedience is not an outdated concept, it is the core value. The sermons are scripture-heavy, often expositional in style. The tone is serious, soul-searching, and deeply convicting. Members are not simply encouraged to grow, they are called to a higher standard.

Repentance is not just present. It is central. The worship is intimate, often quiet, spirit-led, with an emphasis on spiritual cleansing. Community standards are clear: holiness, modesty, maturity, and accountability are expected, not suggested. And those who thrive here do not just want encouragement, they crave challenge.

This is a church for the spiritually disciplined. A place where transformation comes not through motivation, but through submission. Its Member Value Proposition is not entertainment, not ease, not attraction, it is deep discipleship. If you want your faith to be sharpened, your walk to be checked, and your life to be aligned, this is your home.

Lakewood Church: The Culture of Grace, Identity, and Hope
Then there is Lakewood. One of the largest churches in the world, and arguably one of the most controversial, not because of what it does wrong, but because of what it does differently.

Lakewood's culture is centered on grace. It leads with acceptance, affirmation, and the belief that God's love is unconditional and abundant. The preaching style is motivational and life-applying. The atmosphere is bright, joyful, and forward-looking. Rather than centering repentance, Lakewood centers hope, not as a replacement, but as a lens through which everything is framed.

Here, the Christian life is about overcoming. About discovering your purpose. About living in the fullness of God's favor. Lakewood teaches people to speak life, embrace destiny, and understand their identity in Christ as sons and daughters, not as condemned sinners, but as deeply loved individuals.

Community expectations are not focused on how you dress or how much scripture you quote, but on your willingness to grow and walk in faith. The emotional impact is real, Lakewood builds confidence, self-worth, and spiritual boldness. This is not a church built to correct people. It is a church built to empower them.

Two Churches, One Lesson: Culture That Knows Itself Wins

2819 Church and Lakewood Church are not competing in the same space. They are not fighting for the same members. They are not trying to meet in the middle. And that is exactly why both work. They know who they are.

2819 leads with obedience. Lakewood leads with grace. But both are deeply aligned cultures, and that is what makes them effective.

People who want accountability, repentance, and sacred structure know to go to 2819. People who want inspiration, affirmation, and identity-focused encouragement find belonging at Lakewood.

Neither church tries to be all things to all people. They are unapologetic about their values. Their language, rituals, worship styles, and member experiences are all calibrated around those values.

That is strong culture. Not agreement, not popularity, but consistency. You know what you are getting. And for the members who resonate, it feels like home.

When churches, like businesses, align their actions with their beliefs, culture becomes more than atmosphere. It becomes transformation. In the case of these two churches, it becomes ministry that works.

CATEGORY	2819 CHURCH– OBEDIENCE-FOCUSED	LAKEWOOD CHURCH– GRACE-FOCUSED
Member Value Proposition	Be part of a community that challenges you to grow in spiritual maturity, obedience, and accountability to please God.	Experience an environment that uplifts, encourages, and equips you to live confidently in God's grace.
Core Theological Emphasis	Holiness, sanctification, discipline, obedience to God's Word	Grace, acceptance, favor, living in God's love
Primary Success Lens	Depth of discipleship, spiritual obedience, soul transformation	Reach, encouragement, inspiration, positive Christian identity
Spiritual Tone	Reverent, accountability-driven, soul-cleansing	Encouraging, uplifting, hope-filled
Preaching Style	Expository, scripture-heavy, often corrective or instructive	Inspirational, life-applying, often motivational
View of Christian Living	Life of submission and spiritual discipline to grow in Christ	Life of overcoming and receiving God's promises
Repentance Focus	Central — repentance as the foundation of a transformed life	Present — but framed through God's unconditional forgiveness
Worship Atmosphere	Intense, worshipful, spirit-led with space for repentance	Light, Joyful, often celebratory and forward-looking
Community Expectations	High standards of spiritual maturity, accountability, and modesty	Emphasis on personal growth, spiritual encouragement
Emotional Impact	Brings spiritual conviction and reverence	Builds self-worth and spiritual confidence
Foundational Scripture	Matthew 28:19 — "Go therefore and make disciples…"	Romans 8:1 / John 10:10 — "No condemnation… life more abundantly"

NYPD vs. Tokyo Police

Culture in Policing: Command vs. Community, Two Visions of Safety and Authority

We often think about police departments in terms of crime statistics or law enforcement tactics. But just like corporations and churches, policing institutions have cultures. And those cultures shape everything, from how officers carry weapons to how they are portrayed in the media. In this case, we are looking at two dramatically different examples: the New York Police Department and the Japanese National Police based in Tokyo.

On the surface, both are respected law enforcement bodies in major global cities. But underneath, their philosophies about authority, safety, and service come from entirely different cultural worlds. And that difference shows us how deeply culture informs behavior, even in institutions tasked with enforcing the law.

NYPD: The Culture of Command, Visibility, and Control

New York City is fast, chaotic, and dense. Its police force reflects that energy. The NYPD has a culture of visible authority. Officers are armed, trained for pursuit, and expected to respond quickly and assertively in the face of threat or resistance. It is a force shaped by high crime volume and intense public scrutiny.

This is a department that embraces a militarized posture. Officers routinely carry semi-automatic pistols. They use force more frequently than most global counterparts. The philosophy is simple: enforce law visibly, act decisively, and maintain a presence.

The result is mixed. Some communities see the NYPD as a symbol of safety. Others, especially marginalized groups, experience distrust, tension, and fear. Media portrayals often amplify these extremes, placing NYPD in the national spotlight, both as heroes and as targets for critique.

Internally, the structure is complex. Unions protect officers, political oversight influences discipline, and community integration varies widely by precinct. The culture is rooted in American ideals of freedom, individual rights, and self-defense. The Member Value Proposition here is simple: fast response and visible control in the face of real threats. That is what it offers, and for many, that is what they expect.

Tokyo Police: The Culture of Harmony, Prevention, and Quiet Authority

Now shift to Tokyo. Japan's police operate on an entirely different cultural foundation. Instead of high-volume crime response, their approach is built around prevention, trust, and community presence. They carry weapons but rarely use them. They are trained in martial arts and conflict de-escalation. They patrol neighborhoods through small police boxes called kōban, fostering daily contact and long-term familiarity.

Philosophy is not just different, it is deeply cultural. Authority here is quiet, methodical, and relationship based. The use of force is viewed as a failure of communication, not a first response. Policing is not about domination. It is about preserving harmony.

Media rarely criticizes Tokyo police. Public perception is generally positive. Integrity and accountability are embedded through centralized discipline. Officers are seen as helpful, even noble, figures within the community. Their value proposition is not just safety, it is trust. Citizens expect officers to be present, approachable, and morally upright.

Command or Community, the Culture Is What Speaks

These two departments are not just separated by geography. They are separated by worldview.

The NYPD is shaped by urgency and visibility. The Japanese Police by method and restraint. One measures strength in rapid response. The other in quiet presence. But neither is haphazard. Each reflects the values that surround it.

Both function in their contexts. And both reveal this core truth: culture is the compass, even in uniform.

When a policing culture knows its purpose, trains to it, and reinforces it daily, trust or fear, harmony or authority, the outcomes become predictable. Not always perfect, but consistent. Just like in corporations, strong culture in policing is not about style. It is about clarity. When clarity meets consistency, even something as polarizing as law enforcement becomes a model for how culture drives behavior at scale.

NYPD (New York Police Department) vs. Japanese Police

CHARACTERISTICS	NYPD (ASSERTIVE & MILITARIZED)	JAPANESE POLICE - TOKYO (HARMONIOUS & COMMUNITY-BASED)
Customer Value Proposition	Fast, visible response to high-volume crime, prioritizing law enforcement in dense urban settings	Trusted, visible local presence focused on prevention, relationship-building, and community trust
Cultural Approach	Adversarial, rights-focused, crime deterrence	Harmony-driven, community-oriented, non-confrontational
Policing Style	Militarized, visible force, rapid response	Procedural, methodical, de-escalation focused
Crime Rate	Handles high-volume, high-visibility crime in a dense, diverse city	Maintains one of the lowest crime rates in the developed world
Weapon Use	Officers routinely carry semi-automatic pistols and use them with moderate frequency	Officers carry revolvers but rarely use them—minimal firearm discharges annually
Use-of-Force Philosophy	Assertive; uses force in response to resistance or threat	Force is an absolute last resort; heavy emphasis on verbal control
Community Integration	Varies by precinct; often lacks trust in marginalized areas	High trust; kōban (neighborhood police boxes) foster daily contact
Training Focus	Firearms, pursuit, control tactics	De-escalation, martial arts (judo, kendo), community relations
Discipline & Oversight	Complex, with union protection and political oversight	Centralized, with high expectations for integrity and accountability
Public Perception	Mixed to negative, especially in communities of color	Generally positive, seen as helpful and trustworthy
Media Portrayal	Frequently in the spotlight, scrutinized	Rarely in controversy; media often portrays positively
Cultural Influence	Rooted in U.S. values of freedom and individualism	Rooted in collectivism, respect, and social order

U.S. Vs. China

National Culture at Scale: The Individual vs. The Collective, Two Superpowers Shaped by Identity

With 195 countries in the world, few stand as tall or as opposite as the United States and China. On nearly every global ranking, economic power, military reach, cultural influence, these two nations lead the pack. But they do so from completely different cultural foundations.

One is built on the idea of the individual. The other on the power of the group.

This is not just about politics or economics. This is about national identity. It is about culture, values, beliefs, and behaviors that define how people think, act, and relate to one another. And in the United States and China, that cultural contrast is more than visible. It is structural.

The United States: A Culture of Individual Freedom

America was born in rebellion. It declared independence not just from a country, but from control. That spirit of autonomy is baked into its identity. Freedom, personal expression, and the right to choose are more than ideals, they are expectations.

In the American context, success is personal. Citizens are encouraged to stand out, take initiative, speak their minds, and follow their own path. The nuclear family is prioritized. Children are raised to be independent from a young age. Careers are self-driven. Workplace culture celebrates ambition, innovation, and individual performance.

Even in conflict, the American approach reflects this culture. Direct communication is considered honest. Disagreement is not always disrespect. Individual rights are protected fiercely, and leadership is often participative and assertive.

This is a culture that values the self. Its citizen value proposition is the promise of personal freedom, opportunity, and the power to chart your own course.

China: A Culture of Harmony and the Collective

China's cultural foundation is not built on rebellion, but on tradition. The legacy of Confucianism, the weight of history, and the philosophy of harmony have created a national identity centered on interdependence, hierarchy, and social responsibility.

In China, success is collective. It is measured by group progress, family honor, and national strength. Children grow up understanding their role in a larger whole. The extended family is often central. Loyalty, respect for elders, and filial piety are deeply embedded values.

In the workplace, collaboration and humility are praised. Team alignment is emphasized over individual spotlight. Decisions are made through consensus. Communication is often layered, implicit, and context-aware. Even disagreement is handled with care to preserve harmony and avoid causing loss of face.

Leadership tends to be authoritative, but not in a domineering way. It is about long-term trust and stewardship of collective well-being. The citizen value proposition in China is about belonging, stability, and shared progress. It is the assurance that your life matters because it contributes to something greater.

Two Cultures, One Common Lesson: Know Who You Are

The United States and China do not compete because they are the same. They compete because they are different. And they excel not by copying each other, but by leaning into their unique cultural identities.

Individualism produces innovation, expression, and ambition. Collectivism produces cohesion, resilience, and social alignment. Both systems have strengths. Both have flaws. But both demonstrate what happens when a nation fully embodies its culture.

Strong culture, at the national level, is not about which values are better. It is about how clearly those values are defined, and how deeply they are lived.

Whether you are building a company or leading a country, the principle holds: culture only becomes powerful when it is consistent. That consistency creates trust, shapes behavior, and drives performance.

The U.S. and China could not be more different. And yet, they both succeed. Not in spite of their differences, but because of their cultural strength.

CHARACTERISTICS	UNITED STATES– INDIVIDUALIST CULTURE	CHINA–COLLECTIVIST CULTURE
Citizen Value Proposition	Promise of personal freedom, choice, and individual opportunity in all aspects of life	Commitment to collective strength, social contribution, and national pride through group harmony
Moral Lens	Individual rights, personal ethics	Social responsibility, relational harmony
GDP (2023)	~$27.9 trillion USD (World's largest economy)	~$17.7 trillion USD (2nd largest economy globally)
Fortune 500 Companies	136 companies headquartered in the U.S.	142 companies headquartered in China (including Hong Kong)
Military Power	**#1 globally**–largest budget, nuclear triad, global presence	**#2 globally**–rapid modernization, largest standing army, advanced tech
Decision-Making Style	Independent, personal choice driven	Consensus-driven, hierarchy-respecting
Conflict Approach	Direct confrontation is acceptable	Indirect, preserving face and group harmony
Leadership Preference	Participative, assertive, innovation-driven	Respectful of hierarchy, authoritative, long-term loyalty
Communication Style	Low-context–clear, direct, explicit	High-context–implicit, layered, relationship-aware
Success Definition	Personal growth, freedom, success based on individual merit	Group success, social contribution, family or team advancement
Family & Social Focus	Nuclear family, independence at a young age	Extended family, filial piety, generational responsibility
Workplace Culture	Employee initiative, personal goals, self-promotion	Team alignment, collective goals, humility over spotlight

Strong Culture Wins—Even When It's Taboo

Conventional wisdom tells us that religion and business do not mix. In fact, in many professional circles, faith is considered too personal, too polarizing, or simply too controversial for the workplace — especially in profit-driven companies. But what if that very thing — a company's unapologetically clear belief system — is not a liability, but an asset? What if cultural clarity, even when rooted in something taboo, is the real engine of long-term success?

This section makes a bold but evidence-backed claim: any organization, regardless of its values, its sector, or the potential for controversy, can achieve extraordinary success if it is built on a strong culture.

And by strong, we mean what this book has consistently emphasized: a culture that is very specific in defining its shared values, beliefs, norms, and practices, and then behaves with fierce consistency in alignment with those values across every layer of the organization.

It is not about what your values are. It is about how clearly you define them, how deeply you embed them, and how consistently you live them. Chick-fil-A and Al Rajhi Bank are two striking examples — not just because they are religious, but because they are culturally strong. Let us start with Chick-fil-A.

Chick-fil-A: Christian Values, Billion-Dollar Impact

Chick-fil-A is not just a fast-food chain. It is a cultural institution — and one that does not shy away from its roots. Since its founding in 1967 by S. Truett Cathy, the company has been open about its mission: "To glorify God by being a faithful steward of all that is entrusted to us, and to have a positive influence on all who come in contact with Chick-fil-A."

That level of specificity is rare in corporate America. What is even more rare? Their commitment to it.

The most famous example is the chain's refusal to open on Sundays. In an industry where Sunday is often the most profitable day of the week, this move is almost unthinkable. By some estimates, the company forfeits over $1 billion a year in potential revenue because of that one policy. But they have never flinched. Not once. Not even under pressure.

That kind of consistency builds something money cannot buy trust. Customers and employees alike know what Chick-fil-A stands for. And they reward that clarity with loyalty. Chick-fil-A generates more revenue per store than any other fast-food brand in the United States. Its customer service rankings are consistently at the top. Its franchise model is one of the most competitive in the country.

They have built a brand not just on chicken, but on conviction. And that conviction is not performative — it is cultural. It is baked into how they hire, how they train, how they treat people, and how they lead.

Their faith identity is not a hurdle. It is the foundation. And the results speak for themselves.

Al Rajhi Bank: Faith-First Finance That Competes with the World

On the other side of the globe, in a completely different industry, is another example of strong culture in action. Al Rajhi Bank, headquartered in Saudi Arabia, is one of the largest Islamic banks in the world. It operates under Shariah law, which means no interest-bearing loans, no investments in unethical businesses, and a strong focus on social responsibility.

In a Western financial framework, these policies might seem limiting. But inside their context, they create strength. Al Rajhi manages over $220 billion in assets and earns more than $14 billion in annual revenue. That is not a niche institution — that is a global financial powerhouse.

Every product, every service, and every policy is designed around Islamic principles. Transactions are reviewed by a Shariah Board. Employee training includes ethical service delivery, not just technical skills. This is not branding — it is behavioral.

And it works. Al Rajhi customers do not just see it as a bank. They see it as an extension of their beliefs — a place where their financial lives are aligned with their personal values. That creates more than just retention. It creates relationship.

What Chick-fil-A and Al Rajhi Bank Teach Us About Culture

These companies could not be more different in what they do, who they serve, or where they are located. But they share one foundational characteristic: they know who they are, and they live it boldly.

Both Chick-fil-A and Al Rajhi Bank:

- Clearly define what they believe
- Embed those beliefs into every function, from hiring to service to strategy
- Maintain alignment even when it is unpopular or costly
- Succeed because they behave in ways that match what they claim to value

In other words, they are culturally strong. Not because of their faith per se, but because of their cultural integrity. That is what makes them magnetic. Predictable. Trusted.

In a world where many organizations shift with every wind, these two stand firm. And that firmness is exactly what earns them results.

It Is Not About Popularity. It Is About Predictability.

Yes, both Chick-fil-A and Al Rajhi Bank have had their critics. Yes, they have weathered controversy. But the point is not whether people agree with them. The point is that people know what to expect.

That is what strong culture creates — predictability, not perfection. Employees and customers do not have to guess what these companies believe. That confidence turns into competitive advantage.

Strong culture is not reactive. It is proactive. It does not apologize for itself. It shows up every day in what people see, feel, and experience.

So, if religiously rooted organizations can build this kind of success in highly secular industries, what is stopping others from doing the same around their own values?

Culture Is Not About Religion. It Is About Integrity.

Chick-fil-A and Al Rajhi Bank are not successful simply because of faith. They are successful because of clarity. They are consistent. They are authentic. And they are aligned from the inside out.

This is not a chapter about religion. This is a chapter about what happens when culture is not a marketing exercise — but a way of being.

In a noisy world, consistency cuts through. And in organizations where everyone knows the playbook and believes in the mission, excellence follows.

That is the power of a strong culture. It is not about being popular. It is about being known, and being real. And that kind of authenticity? It always wins in the end.

Summary: Lessons on Leading Successful Cultures in Different Environments

Strong culture is not about similarity. It is about sincerity. Across every example in this chapter — whether it was a fast-food chain or a faith-based bank, a global tech empire or a national government — one truth came through again and again. Culture is not about what you believe. It is about how clearly you define it, and how consistently you live it.

From Chick-fil-A and Al Rajhi Bank, we learned that faith-based values can thrive in secular markets when practiced with integrity. From Amazon and Google, we saw that even opposing views of work, productivity versus humanity, can create extraordinary success if embedded with conviction. From Siemens and Virgin, we witnessed that structure and spontaneity both work when tied to purpose. And from the United States and China, we saw that even nations rise on the power of cultural clarity.

What all these institutions have in common is not the type of culture, but the strength of it. They are not always popular. They are not always agreed with. But they are consistent. And that consistency builds trust, shapes behavior, and drives results.

Whether you lead a team, a company, or a country — the takeaway is this: define your culture, align your actions with it, and live it out without apology. Because in a world full of change, culture is the one thing strong enough to hold everything together.

CHAPTER 7

TRANSFORMING CULTURE

Recognizing When Change is Needed

The CEO didn't call me because something was on fire. He called because something felt off.

"Performance is steady," he told me. "But I don't feel momentum. We're hitting our numbers, but just barely. I don't see the energy. I don't hear new ideas. It's like we're succeeding in slow motion."

When I reviewed the data, the pattern was clear. Sales had only increased 2 percent year over year, just enough to claim progress, not enough to inspire it. Turnover among mid-level leaders climbed 18 percent in the past eighteen months. And the succession pipeline? Nearly flatlined. Only 10 percent of internal candidates were marked "ready now" for the roles they were supposed to grow into.

On paper, nothing screamed, emergency. But culture rarely screams. It whispers, it withdraws, it withers.

When I walked through the halls, I saw the symptoms the numbers couldn't show, cautious conversations, safe ideas, emotional disengagement from people who used to care deeply. The company was functional, but not alive. And everyone could feel it.

That's when you know it's time to ask the harder question: What is our culture producing, and what is it costing us?

Here are seven signs your organization's culture may be overdue for reinvention:

7 Signs It's Time to Transform Your Culture

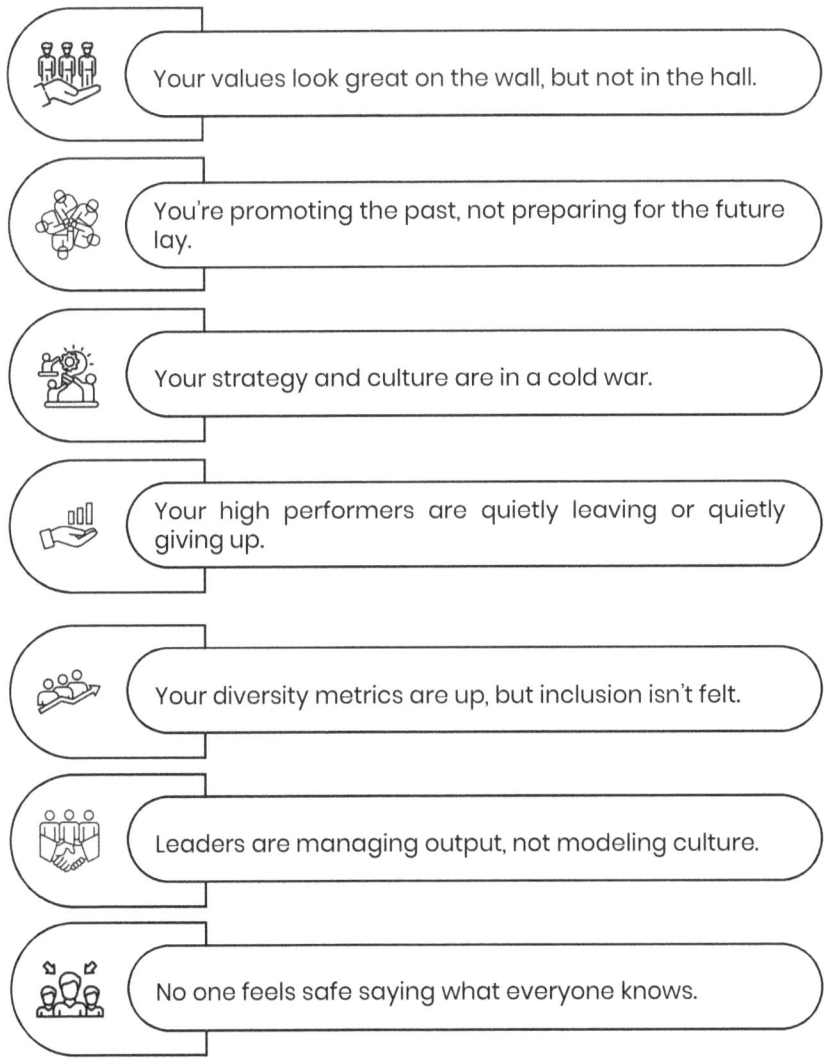

- Your values look great on the wall, but not in the hall.
- You're promoting the past, not preparing for the future lay.
- Your strategy and culture are in a cold war.
- Your high performers are quietly leaving or quietly giving up.
- Your diversity metrics are up, but inclusion isn't felt.
- Leaders are managing output, not modeling culture.
- No one feels safe saying what everyone knows.

7 Signs It's Time to Transform Your Culture:

1. Your values look great on the wall, but not in the hall
2. You're promoting the past, not preparing for the future
3. Your strategy and culture are in a cold war
4. Your high performers are quietly leaving or quietly giving up
5. Your diversity metrics are up, but inclusion isn't felt
6. Leaders are managing output, not modeling culture
7. No one feels safe saying what everyone knows

1. Your values look great on the wall, but not in the hall

You've likely seen it, those five aspirational words engraved in the lobby, recited at company meetings, printed on every slide deck. But when you ask people how those values show up in hiring, in promotions, in conflict, or even in product design, you get a blank stare.

That's not culture. That's decoration.

Culture lives in the behaviors people repeat when no one's watching. If your stated values aren't driving decisions or defining success, they're not alive. And what's not alive eventually dies.

2. You're promoting the past, not preparing for the future

If leadership appointments are based on tenure or likability more than vision and readiness, you're not building a bench, you're building a bubble.

When organizations only reward those who mirror the past, they unintentionally punish those who challenge it. You end up with a leadership team full of legacy behaviors that no longer serve a future-facing strategy. And that gap is where your culture gets stuck.

3. Your strategy and culture are in a cold war

You may have a beautiful strategy, one that demands speed, agility, innovation, and collaboration. But if your culture still rewards hierarchy, caution, control, and competition, then your strategy and culture are quietly fighting each other.

And in that fight, culture always wins.

Until your culture supports the behaviors your strategy needs, transformation efforts will stall. Every time.

4. Your high performers are quietly leaving or quietly giving up

Not everyone rage-quits. Some just fade. They stop bringing new ideas. They stop raising red flags. They stop mentoring. They stop caring.

These are often your most capable people. And their silence is not disengagement, it's self-protection.

When your most invested talent becomes emotionally distant or professionally invisible, it's not because they've changed. It's because the environment has.

5. Your diversity metrics are up, but inclusion isn't felt

Hiring more diverse candidates is a start. But if they don't feel heard, supported, or safe, then you've changed your numbers, not your norms. I've seen organizations celebrate hitting DEI goals on paper while women of color whisper to each other in parking lots about what's really happening. If belonging isn't built into how people lead, decide, and communicate, your culture is performative, not transformative.

6. Leaders are managing output, not modeling culture

If culture is how we do things, then leadership is how we show others how we do things. Culture transformation begins with modeling. That means leaders must embody the behaviors they expect, visibly and consistently.

When leaders manage tasks but avoid coaching, when they push for accountability but resist feedback, when they chase performance without presence, culture erodes from the top down.

7. No one feels safe saying what everyone knows

When your team is talking after the meeting instead of in it, you've got a problem. If people feel safer avoiding truth than confronting it, you're not running a high-performing culture, you're running a highly managed one.

Innovation, trust, and alignment are built in cultures where candor is protected, not punished. If the truth feels like a risk, your culture is already in retreat.

The earlier you recognize these signs, the more options you have to respond. Culture isn't fixed with slogans or swag. It's transformed through clarity, courage, and consistent action, especially when everything looks "fine."

Culture Change Roadmap

So once you know change is needed, then what?

This is where most organizations stall. They know something is off, but they either overreact with surface-level fixes or under-react by kicking the responsibility to HR. Culture work is not about slogans or a new initiative buried in slide 47 of a town hall. It is about transforming how your organization thinks, behaves, and leads, and doing it in a way that aligns with where you're headed, not just where you've been.

The most powerful culture transformations I've seen did not start with a campaign. They started with a courageous decision at the top. A decision to lead differently. To listen more. To confront what's comfortable. And to invite others into something more meaningful.

This roadmap reflects that kind of leadership. It draws on what works, not just in theory but in the lived experiences of real leaders navigating real complexity. We integrate McKinsey's 7S Framework to align strategy, structure, and systems. We apply the ADKAR model to help individuals shift their behavior and sustain change. And we guide leaders through the emotional landscape of transformation using Bridges' Transition Model, recognizing that most resistance to change is not about logic, it's about loss.

Cultural transformation must be led with clarity from the top, activated through the system, and reinforced at every level. Our roadmap follows five essential steps:

1. Lead with Intention, Not Just Authority
2. Diagnose the Truth, Not Just the Data
3. Reimagine the Organization for the Future
4. Activate Change Through Every Layer
5. Reinforce, Sustain, and Evolve

Start at the Top: Lead with Intention, Not Just Authority

Every culture conversation starts at the top, whether leadership realizes it or not. In every organization I've worked with—corporate, civic, nonprofit, or faith-based, the senior team acts as the cultural thermostat. Not the thermometer, which reacts to conditions, but the thermostat, which sets the tone. If the C-suite is cautious, disconnected, or unaccountable, those signals ripple across the entire organization no matter what the PowerPoint says.

That is why cultural transformation can never be outsourced. It must be led. Culture work begins with the senior team not just agreeing that change is needed, but owning the personal work required to model it. That means leaders must go first. They must become the early adopters of the mindset, the behavior, and the energy they want to see across the enterprise.

One of the first things I do with executive teams is ground them in why culture transformation is not just an HR initiative, but a business imperative. That conversation is not soft. It is about performance. Growth. Innovation. Customer retention. Speed. It is about the very things they already care about—but linking them to the often-invisible systems of belief, behavior, and belonging that shape how work actually gets done.

This is also the moment to model what most organizations lack: vulnerability. Executives must be willing to say, "Here is where I have contributed to the problem," or "Here is what I need to unlearn." If culture is going to shift, people need to see their leaders wrestle, evolve, and grow. Otherwise, the transformation reads as compliance, not conviction.

You cannot lead a culture shift with slogans. You lead it with decisions. With calendars. With who you promote and what you tolerate. You lead it with presence. Culture flows from what leaders embody. So, the first move in the roadmap is not launching an initiative. It is choosing to be the living, breathing evidence of the change you are asking others to make.

That is what separates symbolic leadership from cultural leadership. And that is where transformation begins.

Diagnose the Truth, Not Just the Data

You cannot transform what you refuse to see. And yet many organizations skip straight to solutions before they have taken time to fully understand the culture they are trying to change. That is a mistake you cannot afford to make.

Before you start casting vision, reshaping behaviors, or launching new initiatives, you need to get grounded in what is already true. You need to understand how people think, how they move, how they decide, how they avoid, how they perform. Not based on hope, but based on evidence.

That starts by conducting a Cultural Gap Analysis—a structured way of identifying the disconnect between your current culture and the culture required to achieve your strategic goals. To do this well, you need two things: a deep understanding of what is, and a clear articulation of what needs to be. And to get there, you need the right tools.

I recommend combining two frameworks: the McKinsey 7S Model and the STAR Model. Used together, they help you assess both the structural and cultural levers that shape behavior across your organization.

Let's walk through how to apply each of them—step by step.

Step 1: Document Your "Current Culture As-Is"

Start by creating a detailed cultural snapshot. This is not guesswork or a gut feeling. This should be a formal deliverable you create and use as a foundation. At a minimum, this report should include:

- **Cultural Assessment Findings:** Use surveys to gather broad data, but go deeper with interviews, focus groups, and observation. Look for themes, contradictions, and silences. Watch meetings. Sit with frontline staff. See how leaders show up when no one is taking notes.
- **Values and Norms:** Identify not just the stated values, but the unwritten rules. What gets praised? What gets punished? What do people learn quickly without being told? These are your true cultural anchors.
- **Behavioral Patterns:** What behaviors are visible at the team level? Departmental level? Leadership level? What habits have formed over time—and which of them are out of alignment with your goals?
- **Strengths and Frictions:** Where is your culture accelerating the business? Where is it slowing you down? Document both. The goal is not to criticize—it is to understand.
- **Cultural Baseline:** Capture key indicators you can measure again after implementation. These might include engagement metrics, retention data, performance patterns, or inclusion scores.

This "Current Culture As-Is" report becomes your baseline. Without it, you are building change on guesswork.

Step 2: Apply the McKinsey 7S Framework

Once you understand the current state, use the McKinsey 7S Framework to map how your organization functions today—and identify where change is needed. The 7 elements are:

- **Strategy:** What is the business trying to achieve? Is your culture aligned with that direction, or pulling against it?
- **Structure:** How are people organized? Is the structure agile, siloed, flat, hierarchical? What message does it send about power and collaboration?
- **Systems:** What are the formal and informal systems that drive daily work? Think performance reviews, compensation, decision rights, and workflows.
- **Shared Values:** What core beliefs guide behavior? Are they visible in action, or only in messaging?
- **Style**: How do leaders lead? What tone do they set? What behaviors are modeled at the top?
- **Staff:** What skills and demographics define your workforce? Is the culture inclusive of difference, or built around similarity and familiarity?
- **Skills:** What capabilities are strong in your organization? Which are missing? Which are being underutilized or suppressed?

To conduct a full 7S analysis, document both the current state and the desired future state for each "S." Then identify the gaps. For example, if your desired future state requires rapid innovation, but your current structure is risk-averse and approval-heavy, that's a critical gap to close.

I often facilitate workshops with leadership teams where we go through each of the 7 elements line by line. It surfaces the deeper tensions that quick fixes would have overlooked.

Step 3: Layer in the STAR Model

The STAR Model (Strategy, Structure, Processes, Rewards, and People) is especially helpful for identifying the organizational design elements that shape culture through day-to-day operations. Here's how to apply it:

- **Strategy:** Is your strategy clear, and does everyone know how their work connects to it?
- **Structure:** Does your org chart support collaboration, agility, and ownership? Or does it reinforce silos and bottlenecks?
- **Processes:** How are decisions made, how is information shared, and how fast does work flow? Do your internal processes promote speed, trust, and innovation?
- **Rewards**: What behaviors are actually being rewarded? This includes bonuses, promotions, recognition, and informal praise. If you reward the past, you will never build the future.
- **People:** Do you have the right people in the right roles? Do they feel safe, valued, and empowered? Or are they watching and waiting to see if change is real?

Use the STAR Model to examine how each element is influencing behavior. Then ask, "What needs to change here in order for our desired culture to become real?"

Again, document both current and future states. Be specific. For example, you might identify that your current reward system incentivizes individual achievement, but your strategy depends on shared outcomes. That is not a cultural problem, it is a design problem that is shaping culture.

Step 4: Synthesize and Prioritize

Once you've completed both models, combine your findings into a single Gap Map. Identify:

- What needs to stay
- What needs to go
- What needs to evolve
- What systems and behaviors must change first to create visible momentum

Do not try to solve everything at once. Start with the gaps that will have the most impact on credibility and momentum. These become your early transformation priorities.

The organizations that do this well don't just redesign culture. They redesign the conditions that produce it. That means aligning structure, systems, and leadership behaviors with the values they say they want. If you do this work well—thoroughly and truthfully—you will have a roadmap that is not based on trends, but on the lived reality of your organization. And once your people feel seen in that process, they are far more likely to believe in what comes next.

Build the Transformation Strategy

Once you know the truth of where your culture stands, the next step is to design where it needs to go—and how to get there. This is not about launching a culture initiative. This is about reimagining the organization to align with the future you are trying to create.

That means redesigning more than behaviors. It means shifting structure, roles, rituals, and the unwritten rules that shape how people experience power, trust, risk, and belonging every day.

Start by asking one critical question: What kind of culture will make our strategy possible?

Most organizations skip this step and try to push strategy through legacy norms. That is why execution stalls. The culture is still wired for a version of the business that no longer exists.

Here's how to build a transformation strategy that actually works:
Reimagine the Organization

Re-imagination does not start with a mission statement. It starts with structure. Look at your operating model. Are teams organized in ways that support collaboration, agility, and innovation—or are you still working through hierarchy, control, and compliance?

Use the McKinsey 7S Model here again, but this time focused on the future state. Redesign each of the 7 elements—Strategy, Structure, Systems, Shared Values, Style, Staff, and Skills—based on where the organization is going, not where it has been. This becomes your blueprint for organizational alignment.

Then consider the rituals and rhythms of your organization. What meetings reinforce the old culture? What routines could be restructured to support transparency, inclusion, or experimentation? For example, a client I worked with shifted from long monthly updates to weekly stand-ups where every voice was heard. That one change started to shift power dynamics and unlock momentum.

Next, address leadership norms. Many leaders intellectually support change, but still operate with outdated mental models. Do your leaders need to unlearn command-and-control mindsets? Do they need to build new capabilities around coaching, collaboration, and shared accountability? This is where Bridges' Transition Model becomes essential. Your leaders must move through three emotional phases: letting go of old roles and status, navigating the messy middle where clarity is scarce, and stepping into the new way of leading with authenticity. If they don't make that transition, no one else will.

Align Culture with Strategy

Culture is not an accessory to strategy. It is the delivery system.

At this stage, you should be mapping out exactly how your desired culture will support your business goals. That means identifying specific behaviors, habits, and interactions that need to increase, decrease, or evolve in order to bring strategy to life.

For example, if your business strategy depends on speed to market, then your culture must prioritize experimentation, rapid feedback, and decision rights pushed closer to the front line. If your strategy hinges on innovation, but your culture punishes failure, you have a contradiction. Culture must be designed to reinforce the very outcomes your strategy requires.

This is where you define your cultural commitments—the non-negotiables that everyone, especially leadership, must live. These are not vague aspirations. They are clearly stated expectations backed by visible action.

Define Behavioral Anchors

Your new culture must be observable, coachable, and measurable. That requires translating values into behavioral anchors.

For example, "We value collaboration" becomes "We make decisions with cross-functional input before final approval." Or "We value growth" becomes "We expect every people leader to build development plans for their teams, review them quarterly, and integrate coaching into one-on-ones."

These anchors should be embedded into your performance systems, promotion criteria, onboarding, recognition programs, and feedback processes. This is how culture becomes operational, not optional.

The ADKAR model can be used to guide change at the individual level.

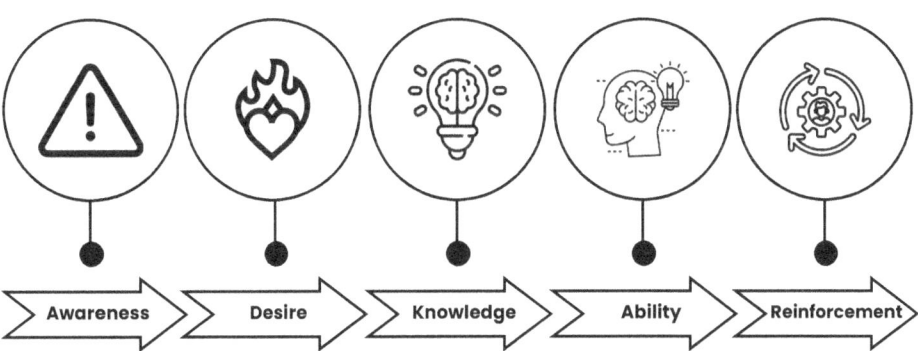

- **Awareness:** Make sure every employee understands why culture change is needed. Communicate the strategic case clearly.

- **Desire:** Help people see what's in it for them. If people do not want to change, they will not.

- **Knowledge:** Teach new behaviors, new tools, and new ways of thinking. Do not assume people know how to operate in the new culture.

- **Ability**: Provide coaching, training, and feedback. Change does not happen through memos. It happens through practice.

- **Reinforcement:** Build it into your systems. Reward what you want to see. Celebrate wins early and often. Measure progress.

Map the End-to-End Culture Journey

Now build your Culture Transformation Roadmap. This is not a one-pager. This is a full change strategy that includes:

- A timeline for when shifts will happen and how they will be sequenced
- Milestones for visible wins and behavioral adoption
- Owners for each workstream of change—structure, systems, leadership, learning, communication
- A measurement plan for tracking change across engagement, behavior, and performance metrics
- Feedback loops and recalibration points

I often advise leaders to build in 30-, 90-, and 180-day checkpoints. Not to measure perfection, but to monitor movement. Are people behaving differently? Are systems reinforcing the change? Are leaders staying consistent or reverting under pressure?

Transformation strategy is not about changing what you say. It is about changing what you tolerate, reward, expect, and model. Do not just ask people to behave differently. Rebuild the organization so that behaving differently becomes the natural, supported, expected way to operate.

This is how culture transformation moves from intention to reality.

Activate the System: From Leadership to Frontline

This is the turning point. Culture transformation becomes real when it moves from words to action. When people begin to see the shift in meetings, decisions, emails, coaching conversations, performance evaluations, and who gets promoted. Culture does not live in intention. It lives in repetition.

At this stage, the goal is to make the culture practical. Tangible. Habitual. Every level of the organization needs to know what the new culture looks like in practice, what is expected of them, and how they will be supported and held accountable for showing up that way.

I often guide organizations through this phase using the ADKAR model. Not as a slogan or framework to display, but as a deeply human way to lead people through change. Awareness. Desire. Knowledge. Ability. Reinforcement. That is the process every person must walk through, whether they are a senior executive or a new hire. If you miss one of those stages, you lose momentum.

Awareness

Begin by helping people understand why the culture must change. Go beyond abstract ideals. Tie the shift directly to business challenges and future strategy.

Examples include

- CEO-led videos and town halls explaining the cost of inaction
- Clear, honest messaging about where the current culture is breaking down
- Discussion guides for managers to help teams process the change

Desire

Once people understand the why, you must give them a reason to care. Involve them. Let them see that their voice matters and their effort will make a difference.

Examples include

- Culture champions chosen from every function and level
- Listening tours, feedback loops, and visible action based on what people share
- Recognition of early adopters who live the new culture in their day-to-day work

Knowledge

Equip your people with the tools and understanding to operate in the new culture. Culture does not change because of posters. It changes because people know what to do differently and how.

Examples include

- Manager toolkits with behavioral expectations and conversation scripts
- Role-specific learning journeys
- Practical examples of how to shift from the old culture to the new

Ability

Let people practice. Make room for mistakes and learning. Give them space to build confidence.

Examples include

- Pilot teams who try out new meeting formats, decision protocols, or recognition rituals
- Peer coaching circles
- Micro-practice scenarios and feedback loops

Reinforcement

This is the most important stage. You must align your systems so that people know the culture is not optional. The fastest way to do that is by linking compensation, promotion, recognition, and consequences directly to cultural behavior.

If someone hits every target but operates in ways that contradict your cultural commitments, they cannot be rewarded in the same way as someone who meets expectations and lives the culture. Culture becomes real when money, access, and opportunity flow through it.

This final part of activation requires three things working together. Reward. Recognition. Accountability.

Build a Culture of Reward, Recognition, and Accountability

People will believe what they consistently see rewarded. They will internalize what gets publicly recognized. And they will ignore what gets quietly tolerated. Rewards, recognition, and accountability are the structural pillars of culture reinforcement. Not through pressure, but through clarity.

Make reward meaningful. Culture should show up in who gets promoted, who gets the bonus, who is tapped for the next project, and who is invited to lead. Cultural alignment must be rewarded just as visibly and consistently as results.

Build reward into

- Performance reviews with weighted scoring for both results and behavior
- Bonus criteria that reflect not just what was delivered but how it was delivered
- Promotion requirements that include feedback from peers and direct reports on cultural alignment
- Access to high-impact opportunities as a reflection of cultural leadership

Make recognition visible and specific. Create ways to spotlight culture in motion so that employees hear and see examples of what the shift looks like.

Build recognition through

- Peer-to-peer nomination systems
- Team-based acknowledgments that reinforce collaboration and shared success
- Leadership meetings that open with a culture spotlight
- Monthly spotlights or newsletters that share real employee examples tied to values

Make accountability just as consistent. Culture only becomes real when misalignment is addressed with courage. Feedback must be clear. Consequences must be consistent. Leaders especially must be held to the standards they ask others to meet.

Ensure accountability through

- Behavior-based documentation in performance reviews
- Follow-up plans for those not modeling cultural expectations
- Leadership evaluations that include cultural criteria
- Reassignment or removal when behavior repeatedly undermines the cultural direction

Reward. Recognition. Accountability. When these are integrated into how you evaluate, compensate, and promote, culture begins to scale. It is no longer aspirational. It becomes operational.

Culture will not sustain itself on good messaging. It will sustain itself through consistent systems. When people see that values lead to opportunity, that behaviors matter as much as results, and that there are real consequences when they do not, they begin to believe. And when they believe, they begin to carry the culture forward.

That is when the shift becomes self-sustaining. And that is when the transformation takes root.

Sustain and Reinforce: Culture Is a System, Not an Event

Culture is only as successful as the goal wins aligned with it. Every meaningful shift in culture reaches a point where the momentum slows. The early energy fades. The champions get tired. The story starts to feel familiar. This is not a failure. This is the nature of change. What matters now is whether the culture you introduced becomes the way the organization actually lives—or a phase people remember.

Sustainability does not depend on charisma. It depends on structure. Culture lasts when it is supported by feedback, measurement, reflection, and correction. Just like strategy, culture must be assessed. Course-corrected. Re-committed. Culture is not a campaign. It is a living system that requires ongoing leadership, alignment, and care.

And most importantly, it must be measured and stewarded at the same level as performance, revenue, participation, and impact. Culture is not soft. It is predictive. It shows up in how aligned your people are with your purpose. How decisions are made. How power is shared. How resilient your teams are when pressure hits. It shows up in retention, inclusion, innovation, community trust, and yes—your numbers.

If you are not monitoring and adjusting your culture with the same rigor you use for financials, programs, or performance, you are leading with one eye closed.

Monitor and Adjust the Cultural System

A healthy culture should evolve. The question is not just whether your culture is improving. The question is whether it is producing the conditions required for your mission to thrive.

Every leadership team should regularly ask three things:

- What needs to increase in our culture right now
- What needs to decrease
- What is working that must be protected and scaled

Sometimes your culture needs more speed. Sometimes more trust. Sometimes more clarity. Sometimes more challenge. Without regular reflection, you will default to habit. And habit is not the same as alignment.

Monitor cultural health the same way you monitor organizational performance. Review your systems, your behaviors, and your outcomes. What do you see repeated in your team meetings, your decision-making, your communication tone? What stories are being told? What do your metrics say? What do your people feel?

The goal is not just cultural stability. It is cultural alignment with your strategy. And that alignment must be checked often.

Measure What Matters Most

Sustaining culture requires meaningful metrics—but not just HR metrics. This is not just about engagement or turnover. It is about whether your culture is actively enabling your mission.

You need to measure cultural performance across the full ecosystem:

- Are your leaders modeling the mindset needed for the future
- Are your values showing up in hiring, decision-making, and budgeting
- Are your systems reinforcing inclusion, accountability, innovation, or whatever your strategy demands
- Are your people equipped and empowered to lead the culture at their level
- Are your clients, members, students, or citizens experiencing your culture in action
- Are your business, performance, or community outcomes being shaped by culture—not in spite of it, but because of it

This kind of measurement is not limited to one dashboard. It is a discipline. It means tracking qualitative signals and quantitative trends. Stories and surveys. Focus groups and performance reviews. It means creating feedback loops that connect frontline experience with executive insight.

And it means paying attention to the edges. Culture shows up most clearly in how you handle tension, conflict, innovation, and growth. If those moments contradict your values, you are not yet living your culture.

Build Feedback and Reflection into Leadership Rhythm

Culture cannot be sustained without honest reflection. Not just at the team level, but at the top. Leadership must create space to ask hard questions, receive unfiltered feedback, and adjust.

You need regular touchpoints that allow you to hear what culture actually feels like. Not just for employees, but for board members, community partners, donors, customers, or whoever your organization serves.

That means creating:

- Listening forums or small group dialogues with every layer of the organization
- Space in leadership meetings to reflect on cultural trends, not just operational KPIs
- Time for strategic storytelling—sharing real examples of when your culture was tested and held
- Leadership reviews that evaluate both outcomes and the cultural integrity of how those outcomes were achieved

Sustained culture does not come from declarations. It comes from leaders asking, "Is this still who we are? Is this still serving us? Where have we drifted?"

That is not weakness. That is stewardship.

Reinforce Through Systems, Symbols, and Story

Culture will not last unless it is seen, felt, and reinforced through every aspect of the organization's rhythm. It must be embedded into how people are hired, trained, rewarded, corrected, and celebrated. But also into the more subtle language of space, story, and ritual.

Look at your environment. What does your space communicate about hierarchy, trust, inclusion, and creativity? What symbols are visible that point to your values? Who is featured in your stories and honored in your language?

Make sure your systems and rituals answer these questions:

- Are we reinforcing the behaviors we say we value?
- Are we celebrating the people who are carrying the culture forward
- Are we challenging the patterns that quietly pull us backward?
- Are we still aligned with the version of ourselves we said we wanted to become?

Culture is not self-sustaining. But it is self-reinforcing—when your systems are clear, your data is honest, and your leadership is reflective. This is not just about keeping momentum. It is about growing in maturity. Organizations that sustain culture well do so because they treat it like any other strategic asset. They listen. They measure. They adjust. And they keep it connected to the reason they exist in the first place.

When culture becomes part of your leadership rhythm—not just your HR rhythm—it stays alive. Not as a program, but as the system that holds your purpose. That is what it means to sustain a transformation. You protect it. You evolve it. And you let it shape everything else.

Summary

Culture is not what you say. It is what you repeat. And in every organization—corporate, civic, nonprofit, government, or faith-based—transformation does not begin with branding. It begins with truth-telling. This chapter mapped out what it takes to lead a real culture shift, not just launch a culture effort.

It begins with recognizing the signals that something must change. Noticing the drift. Listening to what is no longer working. Then leading with intention. If the C-suite does not go first, the organization will not follow. Real culture work requires leaders to confront how they have contributed to the current state and then model something new.

From there, culture transformation must be rooted in a clear understanding of what actually exists. Through structured diagnosis, a current-state assessment, and honest evaluation of values, behaviors, and systems, leaders uncover what is misaligned and what is missing. You cannot transform what you are unwilling to name.

With that insight, leaders reimagine the organization—not just what people do, but how the structure, leadership norms, rewards, and rituals shape behavior. This work is not theoretical. It is systemic. Every level must align: the way people are developed, recognized, held accountable, and celebrated.

The fourth phase is activation—turning the culture into something people can practice. Using tools like ADKAR to bring the change to life across roles, reinforcing expectations through training, rituals, rewards, and consequences. Culture becomes real when it shapes performance, opportunity, and leadership.

Finally, the shift must be sustained through rhythm, not hype. Culture is only as successful as the results it makes possible. That means monitoring what needs to increase, decrease, or stay the same. Measuring what matters. Asking whether culture is still aligned with strategy and still alive in practice. Reinforcing the vision through systems, stories, and symbols so the culture becomes the way the organization operates—not a season it survived.

And at its core, culture must be authentic. Organizations cannot fake alignment for long. A culture that doesn't reflect the real values, voice, and priorities of its leaders and people will eventually collapse under contradiction. Authenticity is not about being perfect. It is about being consistent, honest, and willing to grow. When culture and identity align, trust grows. When culture is performative, trust erodes.

Culture is not a thing to roll out. It is the way your mission walks through people. And when led well, it becomes your most powerful advantage.

CHAPTER 8
THE IMPACT OF THE CORONAVIRUS PANDEMIC ON CULTURE

"I don't know who my people are anymore," the CEO said to me, eyes strained behind the glow of a laptop screen. "They're loyal. They're talented. But they've changed. And if I'm honest, I think I have too."

He wasn't talking about turnover. This wasn't a complaint about remote work or employee engagement. This was a moment of clarity. What he was observing in his team was something he hadn't yet named in himself: cultural disorientation. The pandemic had stripped away the familiar scaffolding of the workplace, and what was left behind wasn't just a new schedule or different tools, it was a new set of values. A different rhythm. A quieter, more spiritual discomfort that wasn't going away just because offices were reopening.

And this wasn't unique. Leaders across industries were experiencing the same realization. They weren't returning to the same organizations. They were returning to people who had reimagined their lives, re-evaluated their relationships, and reshaped what they believed mattered most. The pandemic didn't just change behavior. It rearranged the inner landscape.

Precursors to a Culture Ready to Shift

The pandemic didn't start this shift, it accelerated it. Like water pressing against a dam that was already cracked, COVID didn't cause the rupture. It revealed it. Before the first lockdowns, our culture was already stretched thin, fatigued by overwork, and quietly wrestling with meaning. You could feel it in late-night texts from burnt-out executives, in young professionals quietly exiting high-paying roles, and in the unspoken ache of people who couldn't remember the last time they felt joy.

Pre-pandemic Fatigue and Fragmentation

Culturally, we were running on fumes. Work had become our identity, and productivity our worth. We had convinced ourselves that faster was better and connection could be simulated through Wi-Fi. And while technology had expanded access, it hadn't expanded belonging. People were living publicly but feeling privately invisible. The cracks were already visible. The pandemic just pulled back the curtain.

Digital Dependency Was Already Growing

Digital culture was already creeping in. Slack and Teams had replaced hallway conversations. Instagram became a place to curate life rather than live it. But even then, there was resistance. Remote work, flexible schedules, digital-first cultures, these were fringe practices. Not yet normalized. What the pandemic did was force every organization, every school, every spiritual community to confront what had once been optional. Suddenly, the digital was not an add-on. It was the stage.
Cracks in Trust and Connection

And in terms of trust, we had already been moving from centralized authority to peer-based validation. Influence wasn't flowing from institutions; it was emerging from networks. People trusted what felt real, not what was credentialed. That shift, once subtle, became seismic during COVID. And that would become one of the deepest cultural transformations we are still reckoning with today.

The Pandemic as a Cultural Earthquake

Collapse of Institutional Trust

In the United States, the pandemic revealed just how fragile the trust between people and institutions really was. Early mixed messages from government leaders and public health officials eroded public confidence. Do not wear a mask. Do wear a mask. It is just two weeks. It may be much longer. The contradictions were not just logistical. They were existential. And in the absence of a consistent voice, the public filled the void with doubt.

Science became politicized. Education became a battlefield. Even hospitals and doctors, once sacred and trusted, became subjects of suspicion. People turned to online communities, spiritual influencers, and peer networks for answers. Not because they lacked intelligence, but because they lacked trust.

What used to be a baseline assumption, trust the experts, was replaced with a new, more guarded posture: trust what I can see, feel, or validate for myself. This was not simply a political shift. It was a cultural evolution from passive consumption to active discernment. And in that space, leaders had to learn: trust is not inherited. It is observed. It is earned. And once it is lost, it is hard to rebuild.

Grief and Spiritual Dislocation

Globally, the pandemic introduced a level of grief we had no rituals for. It was not just the loss of life. It was the loss of normalcy, the loss of rhythm, the loss of physical presence in sacred moments. Weddings on FaceTime. Funerals on Zoom. Birthdays without hugs. We grieved in silence, often alone, in bedrooms and bathrooms and in the space between video calls.

Time itself lost structure. The days blurred. The months felt suspended. People forgot how to mark meaning because the rituals that once held time together, holidays, graduations, Sunday services, family dinners, were canceled or digitized. Even those who did not lose loved ones experienced loss, of community, of clarity, of feeling seen.

Grief became layered and nonlinear. One day you would feel a strange, small joy, and the next you would cry over the sound of silence. The disorientation was not just emotional. It was spiritual. When familiar structures fail, the soul starts looking for new ground to stand on. And in that search, many people reached inward. Others reached outward, toward nature, toward meditation, toward ancestral wisdom, toward art.

We did not only lose people. We lost the rites that teach us how to carry loss. When the rituals that mark time go quiet, the soul improvises. That is why so many reached for meditation, long walks, breathwork, prayer, and creative practices they had neglected. Research on virtual funerals and pandemic-era mourning underscored this. Remote participation preserved connection but often complicated grief, leaving many without the embodied closure they needed. Culture work must therefore include ritual work. Design small, repeatable practices where people can process, honor, and re-enter. Do not announce wellness. Build it into the week.

One pastor I worked with summed it up after a Sunday of livestreaming: "We counted views, not faces, and my members grieved alone." He thought his problem was technology. It was ritual. Leaders today must see what he saw: when rituals disappear, the community frays.

The pandemic thinned the veil between the visible and the invisible. And in doing so, it opened space for a deeper, slower, more contemplative culture to emerge beneath the surface. Leaders who honor that inner life in how they structure time, meetings, and recovery will keep the people everyone else is trying to poach.

The Great Reprioritization

One of the loudest cultural aftershocks of the pandemic was not something that could be measured in job losses or economic downturns. It was what happened inside people. There was a deep, internal reordering, a forced confrontation with priorities. Work, once the centerpiece of identity and ambition, lost its shine. People began asking different questions. Not "What do I do?" but "Who do I want to become?" Not "How do I get ahead?" but "Is this still worth it?"

This shift was mislabeled by some as laziness or entitlement. But those of us paying attention knew better. What emerged was not a refusal to work. It was a refusal to keep pretending. People did not just leave jobs. They left the emotional contracts that came with them, the quiet deals they had made to sacrifice health for hustle, time for approval, joy for status. And once they left, they did not want to come back the same way. The Great Reprioritization was not a rebellion. It was a revelation.

The data bears this out. Roughly seven in ten workers say their sense of purpose is defined by work. When purpose is absent, performance and loyalty lag. Conversely, when people experience belonging, performance rises dramatically and turnover risk drops by half. Flexibility remains the loudest proof of respect, with the vast majority of workers wanting control over when they work and a strong majority wanting control over where they work. Stop pretending this will regress to 2019. It is the new psychological contract. Lead accordingly.

And it was not just professionals in high-rise buildings or tech startups who felt this shift. It was teachers, nurses, pastors, and small business owners. People who had always given more than they received. People who were told they were essential but treated as expendable. The pandemic lifted the curtain on what people had normalized. And once you see your worth, you cannot unsee it.

So they chose differently. Not always more comfortably. But more aligned. People moved closer to family. They chose slower-paced jobs. They started businesses that felt meaningful. They downsized to simplify. They logged off from roles that expected everything and gave very little back.

The American Dream, once defined by accumulation, was now being rewritten by alignment. Success started to sound more like, "I'm finally breathing again." Health became more important than hustle. Time became more sacred than titles. And values became louder than fear. For organizations, this meant that culture could no longer be performative. It had to be lived. It had to feel honest. It had to honor what people discovered about themselves in the dark.

Blurred Lines. Global Eyes.

Global Empathy, Global Screens

The world watched itself suffer. Italy's balconies. India's oxygen crisis. New York's emptiness. These images became global windows into collective grief and courage. Never before had so many people witnessed the suffering of others at the exact same time, across borders, cultures, and time zones. Screens became sanctuaries. Smartphones became cathedrals of compassion.

We did not all experience the pandemic equally, but we experienced it together. It created a strange kind of proximity. A shared vulnerability. It was a quiet recognition that despite language and geography, we are all human. That realization was not sentimental. It was anchoring. It was humbling. It was sobering. And it changed the way we witnessed, remembered, and cared.

Cultural narratives across continents began to intersect. The sorrow of one country reverberated in the hearts of another. Even entertainment paused to allow space for silence, for tribute, for stillness. This kind of collective empathy had been theorized in academia, but during

COVID, it was lived. It was the sound of singing on balconies. The image of overrun hospitals broadcast in real time. The viral stories of nurses sleeping in cars and children waving at grandparents through windows.

This was not news. It was human memory being made. And the screens that so often had isolated us suddenly connected us. We were all witnesses. And being a witness changes you. It makes you accountable. It makes you more open. And in many cases, more kind.

Migration and Identity Shift

Remote work untethered people from cities, countries, and even careers. What once seemed immovable, a job location, a family home, a sense of national belonging, now felt optional. Americans began to question not just where they lived, but why. Post-pandemic, there was a growing trend of U.S. citizens relocating abroad not for luxury, but for values. Cost of living, public safety, healthcare access, and cultural alignment drove migration decisions.

New communities of American expats emerged across Portugal, Mexico, Costa Rica, and Spain. They were not tourists. They were seekers. Looking for quality of life, for rhythm, for something that felt more livable. This shift signaled something deeper than logistics. It reflected a changing identity. People were no longer rooted solely in birthplace. They were rooted in alignment, in resonance, in spirit.

Gallup found that by 2023, nearly 17 percent of Americans expressed a desire to permanently move abroad, with the number even higher among millennials and Gen Z. The reasons cited were not primarily political. They were existential. People wanted to live in cultures that prioritized community over consumption, rest over rush, health over hustle. For leaders, the lesson is not about relocation. It is about recognition. Your best talent may be willing to move—or leave—if your culture feels misaligned with what they now value most.

A globalized sense of self took shape. One that was digitally connected, spiritually seeking, and culturally fluid. The idea of "home" became more internal than external. And with that came a new kind of global citizen. Someone who might be raised in Texas, work for a German firm, live in Bali, and attend a virtual church based in Atlanta. This wasn't escapism. It was an embodiment. And it is reshaping how we think about place, purpose, and belonging.

Global Belonging Over Nationalism

As borders closed, a surprising thing happened. People looked beyond them. The crisis showed the limitations of nationalism in solving global problems. Climate change. Pandemics. Economic collapse. These issues were bigger than any one country. And the cultural response reflected that.

People began identifying more with shared values than national flags. Social movements spanned continents. Art, music, and even grief became viral in the truest sense of the word. A poem written in Lagos could comfort someone in London. A protest in Minneapolis could mobilize action in Paris.

The language of belonging began to shift. It was no longer about citizenship. It was about connectedness. People found spiritual homes in global conversations. Non-governmental organizations saw a surge in participation and donations, especially those focused on global health and justice. Social media became both a gathering place and a classroom. People taught each other, held each other accountable, and built communities that did not require visas.

This shift did not erase cultural identity. It expanded it. You could be both proudly Ghanaian and deeply committed to climate action in the Amazon. You could be Southern and still host weekly Zoom calls with friends in Nairobi. The binary of national pride versus global concern began to dissolve. What remained was a more nuanced, more spacious identity rooted in love, justice, curiosity, and shared humanity.

That is the future of belonging. Not bounded by borders but expanded by empathy. Not limited to what you were born into but grown through what you choose to care about. That kind of belonging is not passive. It is built. It is chosen. It is lived.

Global belonging does not ignore history. It honors it. It does not diminish local cultures. It uplifts them within a wider constellation. It is a belonging that listens more than it speaks. It reaches without rushing. And for many emerging generations, it is becoming the default way of seeing the world. Not in opposition to national heritage, but as an evolution of human connection.

This is not just a trend. It is a cultural and spiritual shift toward recognizing that in the face of global crises, it is not enough to be alone. We need each other. We need shared purpose, shared space, and shared stewardship. And that is what global belonging begins to cultivate. Not just an identity, but a practice of humanity itself.

A Leader's Cultural Mandate

With this new era of global unity, driven by technological advancements including social media, comes the opportunity for anyone to become a leader in an instant. A twelve-year-old girl in a small town like Hum, Croatia can have just as loud a voice and paralleled influence as a seasoned executive in Tokyo or New York City. The ability to shape global culture is widening beyond our measure or control. This decentralization of influence only heightens the responsibility of leaders to intentionally navigate culture and the influences on culture within their own organizations.

If your people see themselves as global citizens, your culture must stretch. Meeting rhythms must consider time zones. Decision-making must reflect cross-cultural intelligence. Recognition must celebrate values, not just metrics. And leaders must hold the tension: your organization is no longer just local. It is a node in a global network of values, belonging, and influence. How you steward that responsibility will determine not just retention, but relevance.

Summary

The pandemic did not create a new culture, but it accelerated one that was already forming beneath the surface. Before the world shut down, individuals were quietly questioning their pace, purpose, and sense of belonging. COVID cracked the illusion of stability and exposed how thinly stretched people and institutions had become.

Trust in authority collapsed, not because people stopped caring, but because they began demanding lived authenticity. Grief went unprocessed, with rituals erased or digitized, leaving leaders to rediscover the power of intentional practices that help people metabolize loss and meaning. The Great Reprioritization reordered priorities at both the personal and organizational level. Work became a moral decision, not just an economic one. Flexibility became sacred. Belonging shifted from optional to essential, and purpose became the new currency of loyalty.

Globally, migration patterns signaled that people were no longer tethered by geography but by values. Home became more internal than external, and a new identity as global citizens began to emerge. Screens once seen as isolating became sanctuaries of compassion. Belonging expanded beyond borders into shared values, shared grief, and shared stewardship. National pride did not disappear, but it was held alongside a more expansive sense of human connection.

For leaders, this chapter marks a decisive line in the sand. It is no longer enough to build culture through slogans or structure. Trust must be embodied, not branded. Rituals must restore meaning, not just mark milestones. Culture must reflect what people now deeply value: flexibility, purpose, and wellness. Belonging must be intentionally designed across formats, from the hallway to the Zoom call to the global conversation.

Leadership itself has changed. It is not only technical or strategic. It is cultural, emotional, and spiritual. People are following leaders not just for what they know, but for who they are and how they live what they say. The most effective leaders in this new era are not simply directing operations. They are interpreting culture, curating meaning, and stewarding trust.

The pandemic revealed that influence is no longer inherited. It is lived. Culture is no longer a backdrop. It is the stage. And the leaders who understand this will not only keep their people, they will guide them into futures where work, belonging, and humanity are no longer at odds but aligned.

CHAPTER 9

GENERATIVE AI AND ITS IMPACT ON CULTURE
THE NEW PRESENCE IN THE ROOM

I had just finished presenting to a senior leadership team, including the CIO, CHRO, and a few line-of-business heads. The CIO leaned forward, visibly energized, and said, "We just rolled out a generative AI assistant across customer service. It is already drafting 70 percent of client communications. Our NPS is up. Costs are down. This is going to be everywhere."

The room buzzed. Except for one. The CHRO sat still. Watching.

Later, in the hallway, she pulled me aside. "I am all for innovation," she said. "But I can already feel it. Our people are talking less. They are sending what the system writes. The human part of work is starting to fade, and no one is asking what that means in the long term."

She was right to pause. Something bigger had just entered the organization. Not just a tool. A presence. Generative AI does not simply speed up tasks. It reshapes how people think, how they express themselves, how they collaborate, and how they experience value. It is already writing news articles, generating marketing content, assisting in courtrooms, producing lesson plans, composing music, and developing entire video games. It can write a script, animate the scene, and voice the characters without human help.

That is not theoretical. That is this year.

At the societal level, generative AI is changing what is real, what is trusted, and what is possible. We are entering a time when the difference between fact and fabrication is harder to detect. Creativity can be simulated. Misinformation can be manufactured and scaled with terrifying precision.

It is also breaking barriers. People who do not code are building apps. People who do not write are creating full publications. Students are learning in personalized, dynamic ways. Artists are remixing mediums once out of reach. Productivity is being redefined across industries, regions, and generations.

And then there is the shadow.

Jobs will be lost. Roles will collapse. Social trust will erode in places where the human touch has been replaced with plausible automation. Industries will divide between those who adapt and those who are automated. Education, media, healthcare, and government will all be asked to deliver faster, cheaper, and smarter, often with fewer humans in the loop.

This is not about whether AI is good or bad. It is about what happens when intelligence is no longer human-exclusive.

So what does that mean for your organization? What does that mean for culture, for what people believe, how they belong, what they trust, and how they contribute?

That is where we are going next.

Humanity vs. Efficiency: What Will Remain Sacred

There's a question every organization has to answer now, even if it doesn't ask it out loud:

What parts of our culture are irreplaceable, and what parts are just routine?

That question used to be philosophical. Now it is operational. And you don't get to ignore it.

Generative AI is already reshaping the way work flows through your organization. It is rewriting reports, drafting strategies, coaching in real time, replying to emails, summarizing meetings, pulling sentiment out of surveys, even spitting out new product names while you sleep. There are tools that will finish your sentences and mimic your tone. There are tools that will conduct an interview and screen for values alignment before a human ever sees a résumé.

It is fast. It is competent. It is deeply helpful.

But it is not human.

And no matter how many APIs you plug in, no matter how many LLMs you layer on top, it cannot be. That's where the line must be drawn. Not to stop the tools, but to protect the soul of the place you're building.

Because AI can write a beautiful condolence message, but it cannot sit with you in silence when there are no words. It can suggest a team celebration, but it cannot feel the pride rising in your chest when your team pulls it off. It can remind you that your colleague's mother passed away last week, but it won't pause the meeting to ask how they're doing before diving into the deck.

AI may grow incredibly skilled at simulating care. It may track burnout, suggest breaks, even send your favorite affirmation on your birthday. But here's the difference: you were not created to be noticed. You were created to be known.

There's a difference between recognition and relationship. Between response and presence. Between connection and communion. AI can talk to you. It cannot be with you.

And the parts of your culture people remember and protect are born not from efficient delivery of sentiment, but from the messy, sacred act of one human giving another a moment of their full self.

Automate the noise. But never deceive yourself into thinking you can automate care.

Culture Under Automation: The Shift Employees Feel First

In most organizations, AI enters quietly. Leaders focus on performance. Employees notice presence.

It begins with small things: onboarding messages that feel generic, feedback that sounds templated, recognition that seems strangely polished. At first it feels efficient. Eventually it feels hollow.

People begin to ask themselves, Do they even see me? Did my manager really mean that? Do I matter here, or just my productivity?

I watched this unfold with a leadership team that introduced AI into their internal communications stack. The AI drafted updates, celebrated wins, nudged managers to recognize their people. On paper, nothing was wrong. But employees described the culture as distant. They could not quite name why. Everything sounded right. But no one felt present. That is what leaders often forget: automation does not just speed things up. It replaces the moment. And some moments should not be replaced.

Culture begins to shift the moment employees doubt that what they are experiencing is real. Once that doubt sets in, they do not always leave. But they detach. Quietly. Emotionally. Spiritually. And when they stop offering what cannot be measured, culture begins to hollow out from within.

The Risks, Tradeoffs, and Guardrails

When I finished presenting to another senior team, the CFO was glowing over the numbers. But a director confided afterward, "The energy feels different. People are quieter. It's like we've put a filter between us."

That is the cultural risk of AI: the gains are obvious, the losses are quiet. AI dazzles with speed but struggles with truth. It can fabricate with confidence, leaving leaders to repair credibility. It does not eliminate bias; it codifies it. It can make misinformation feel normal, turning confusion into atmosphere.

And misinformation is no longer theoretical. Deepfakes and synthetic voices are entering mainstream life, eroding trust in what people see and hear. Employees do not leave this at the office door. When a video of a leader can be faked, or when a public statement can be cloned and distributed with no evidence of origin, skepticism seeps into every interaction. If people begin to doubt what is real in society, they eventually begin to doubt what is real in their workplace. Leaders must realize they are not just competing for attention. They are competing for credibility. And in the age of deepfakes, credibility is culture's most fragile currency.

AI also drains resources invisibly, straining power grids, consuming water, and impacting local communities in ways employees notice when your stated commitments to sustainability seem to stop at convenience.

And it is already reshaping economies. Entire roles are shrinking, often for those who can least afford the loss. Productivity gains accumulate to those who own the systems, not those displaced by them. When workers feel unnecessary, it doesn't just change income. It changes identity. Desperation is not a technical bug. It is a cultural fracture.

Perhaps most dangerous is how AI shifts voice. I have seen managers defer to outputs they did not believe, simply because the system sounded smarter than them. That silence costs more than a mistake. It costs courage.

The best AI strategy is not written in code. It is written in conviction. Define what will never be automated. Train teams not only to use AI but to interpret it, question it, and slow it down when wisdom is at risk. Publish the boundaries as clearly as the ambitions.

AI will make organizations faster. It will not make them wiser. Wisdom is still human work. And no efficiency chart can protect a culture that forgets that.

From Code to Culture: Algorithms Reflect Who You Are

Leaders love to believe AI is neutral. Objective. Clean. It is not.

AI is not invention. It is reflection. It learns from your language, your habits, your blind spots. It repeats your culture with scale and polish.

I watched a company pilot AI to support promotions. The goal was fairness. The result was repetition. Old patterns embedded in reviews and ratings were amplified. The same types of people advanced. Employees quickly understood leadership had not confronted the culture, they had automated it.

AI does not invent your culture. It encodes it. And once it encodes it, it plays it back to you faster than you can keep up. If your system rewards sameness, your AI will too. If your leadership assessments penalize dissent, your AI will learn to recommend compliance.

The question is not whether the system is wrong. The question is whether you had the courage to change before it started learning from you.

Voice, Power, and the Myth of Objectivity

I have been in rooms where AI outputs were read aloud, and no one responded. Not because they agreed, but because it felt futile to question the system. It sounded smarter. Cleaner. Neutral.

That is the myth of objectivity. Data feels untouchable. But no algorithm is neutral. It is trained on history, shaped by human imperfection. When organizations start to treat the tool as referee, voice goes quiet. People withdraw. The result is not just silence, but surrender.

Leaders must never abdicate responsibility to the system. AI may inform decisions, but only people can feel their impact. Only people can hold tension, rebuild trust, or wrestle with fairness. If leaders defer too much, they risk building a culture where disagreement is inefficient and truth is automated.

Human-Centered, AI-Enabled: Protecting Your Culture

The invitation is not to resist AI, nor to surrender to it. It is to integrate with intention.

When I work with executive teams, I ask: What are you unwilling to automate? The room is often silent at first. They have thought about what is possible, but not about what is sacred.

That is where strategy begins. With the conviction to keep feedback, recognition, coaching, and moral judgment human-led. With the discipline to slow the cycle when decisions are relational or identity-based. With the courage to design guardrails that protect dignity as fiercely as they pursue efficiency.

AI can free people from distraction so they can connect more deeply. But if left unchecked, it flattens the texture of culture into something efficient but soulless. The future belongs to leaders who will use AI to clear space for the one thing only humans can do: build meaning with each other.

The Economic Earthquake: When AI Widens the Gap

The promise of AI is prosperity. But not everyone will rise with it.

The middle class has been shrinking for decades, and AI risks accelerating the slide. Tasks once seen as secure—clerical work, logistics, paralegal research—are being thinned. Productivity climbs, but participation drops. More output, fewer workers. More wealth, concentrated in fewer hands.

That is not only an economic problem. It is a cultural one. Cultures fracture when people believe they are no longer needed. When dignity is detached from contribution, identity begins to unravel. History tells us: people who feel irrelevant do not fade quietly. They organize. They resist. They destabilize.

This is why conversations about universal basic income and new safety nets matter. Not as ideology, but as cultural stewardship. If machines generate the wealth, people must still have pathways to belonging, to dignity, to purpose. A culture that optimizes efficiency while ignoring equity is not sustainable. It may function for the elite. But it will not hold together.

Rituals, Relationships, and What AI Cannot Replace

The real fabric of culture is not woven through dashboards or statements. It is held in rituals. In the quiet ways people welcome, remember, grieve, and celebrate. In the pauses that say, you matter here.

AI will never master this. Not because it lacks intelligence, but because it lacks intention. Rituals are meaning in motion, and meaning cannot be automated.

The danger is not that AI will forget to send the birthday message. It is that leaders will assume the message is enough. People do not stay for reminders. They stay for relationships. They stay for the unscripted care that no model can simulate.

Culture endures in the moments where presence matters more than performance. A manager asking, "What are you proud of this week?" A leader writing a thank-you note without a template. A team pausing to honor the invisible contributions that kept them afloat.

These are not inefficiencies. They are the memory of the organization. And they cannot be outsourced.

Summary: Generative AI and Its Impact on Culture

Generative AI is not just a technological shift. It is a cultural one. It introduces a new presence into the room—one that changes not only what gets done, but how people feel as they do it.

AI will elevate productivity, creativity, and access. But it will also introduce new risks: bias at scale, misinformation as atmosphere, erosion of voice, deepfakes that blur trust in reality, widening inequality, and rituals replaced with simulations. The organizations that thrive will not be those who adopt the fastest, but those who adopt the most intentionally.

The question is not whether AI will transform culture. It already has. The question is whether leaders will protect what is sacred: trust, belonging, discernment, dignity, and presence.

AI can amplify your efficiency. Only humans can carry your wisdom. And it is wisdom, not speed, that sustains a culture worth belonging to.

CHAPTER

THE DEATH OF DIVERSITY IN THE US?

I had just wrapped up a strategy session with a C-suite team at a major U.S. corporation. The room carried a tension that hadn't fully surfaced during the meeting, but it sat in the silence as people gathered their laptops and shuffled toward the door. As the group filtered out, the Chief Operating Officer lingered. She didn't sit. She didn't smile. She waited until we were the only ones left in the room.

"Can I ask you something off the record?" she said.

I nodded. These are the moments that matter most.

"I don't even know what I'm allowed to say anymore," she admitted. "Half my team wants us to double down on equity. The other half is sending me articles about DEI being illegal. People are getting fired just for saying the wrong thing. I believe in this work, Lepora. I always have. But I also have a company to protect. What am I actually supposed to do?"

This wasn't fear of her team. It was fear of the story. She wasn't navigating just employee expectations or board politics. She was stuck inside a larger cultural shift, one that was now being shaped by law, fear, headlines, and power. The stakes had changed.

Just a week earlier, former President Trump had declared that if re-elected, he would dismantle DEI efforts across the country. He called diversity programs corrupt, dangerous, and un-American. It was not just a policy position. It was a declaration of war. Within days, the ripple effect began. Diversity executives were quietly let go. Equity budgets were frozen. Public institutions scaled back entire teams. And in private meetings like this one, leaders began asking questions they never thought they would have to ask.

This leader wasn't confused about her values. She was clear. But in a moment where even using the word diversity felt like a risk, she did not know how to express them without jeopardizing her credibility, her influence, or the organization she had been entrusted to lead.

That is when I realized we were no longer asking the old question—how do we make diversity work.

Now we were facing a new one.

Does diversity even have a future in the United States?
Are we witnessing its death?
Or are we finally approaching a necessary transformation?

This chapter is about that reckoning. It is not just about what diversity has been. It is about what it is becoming. And who we are becoming in response to it.

Definitions of Diversity: What Diversity Is and Isn't

Before we talk about the death or transformation of Diversity in the U.S., we need to get honest about what we are even talking about. Too often, people use diversity, equity, and inclusion interchangeably—as if they are different shades of the same strategy. They are not. These are distinct cultural concepts, with different implications, different expectations, and very different levels of risk. If we are going to have a real conversation about what is happening in this country right now, then we have to separate the language from the slogans and deal with the substance underneath.

Diversity is difference. Not general difference, but difference as it relates to identity, experience, perspective, and presence. Diversity in the U.S. is about who is in the room. It is a headcount issue. It is the makeup of the team, the leadership table, the candidate pool, the client portfolio. Diversity tracks race, gender, generation, sexual orientation, religion, ability, socioeconomic background, and other dimensions of identity that have shaped people's opportunities and worldviews. It is visibility. It is representation. It is a number—and, when done well, it is a signal of what that number means.

Equity is access and accountability. Equity is not about who is in the room. It is about how the room works. Who gets invited to speak. Who gets funded? Who gets promoted? Who gets heard? Equity interrogates systems and policies. It addresses how resources and power are distributed and works to close the gaps that have been created by history, bias, and design. Equity is not neutral. It is corrective. That is why it makes so many people uncomfortable. It asks organizations to look at what they have privileged and what they have ignored. It requires a realignment of structures, not just sentiments.

Inclusion is belonging and participation. It is not a count. It is a climate. Inclusion is the condition under which people feel they can show up fully and contribute meaningfully. It is measured not by numbers but by experience. Do people feel safe here? Do they feel heard? Do they feel needed, or merely tolerated? Inclusion is what makes diversity sustainable. Without it, difference becomes tokenism. And without equity, inclusion becomes hospitality with no power.

Each of these—diversity, equity, and inclusion—requires different muscles. They demand different mindsets. They draw on different disciplines. Diversity is a function of design. Equity is a function of justice. Inclusion is a function of culture. To collapse them into one vague initiative is to guarantee failure.

And yet this is exactly what many organizations have done.

So the question becomes: why?
Why do some leaders lean into diversity but avoid equity?
Why do others embrace inclusion but resist representation?

Because each of these words touches a different center of gravity. Diversity in the U.S. touches identity. Equity touches power. Inclusion touches culture. And that is where the tension lives.

Diversity feels manageable. It can be tracked, benchmarked, and presented on a slide. It is visible. It gives the appearance of progress. Equity, on the other hand, feels disruptive. It calls out legacy systems and demands redistribution—of time, of opportunity, of attention. And inclusion feels personal. It is intimate and subjective. It is harder to standardize. But all three are required for any culture that wants to be whole.

If we misunderstand the differences between these terms, we will misunderstand the resistance they provoke and the transformation they require. The death of Diversity in the U.S. is not just about political backlash. It is about a collective failure to define, to differentiate, and to deliver on the promises we keep making.

The Cultural Paradox: Conformity Builds Culture. Diversity Disrupts It?

Culture, by nature, is cohesive. It is built on repetition, shared assumptions, and a deep sense of how things are done around here. Strong cultures thrive on alignment. They rely on behaviors that are modeled, repeated, and reinforced over time. Whether those behaviors are spoken out loud or carried silently, they form the glue that holds people together. That is what makes a culture feel strong—it has direction, rhythm, predictability. It gives people a sense of belonging because they know what is expected and what will be accepted.

That same cohesion is what makes a team move fast. It reduces the need for constant clarification. People finish each other's thoughts. They share mental models. Decisions flow quickly because values are implicit and assumptions are shared. This is the gift of conformity. It makes culture efficient, scalable, and emotionally safe—for those already inside of it.

Diversity, however, disrupts all of that.

Diversity introduces contradiction. It brings in different identities, different perspectives, different ways of thinking and communicating. It calls into question the very norms that culture depends on functioning smoothly. Where a cohesive

culture tends to run on instinct; a diverse culture runs on inquiry. What was once automatic now requires explanation. What was once assumed now needs to be examined. What was once united in rhythm now pulses with friction.

This is the paradox that too few leaders are willing to name. Diversity in the United States is a cultural force—but it is not a comforting one. It stretches. It challenges. It requires something more than surface-level slogans or headcount metrics. A truly diverse culture is not an aesthetic upgrade. It is a structural transformation. It does not offer immediate comfort or simplicity. It invites tension. It forces decisions. And it exposes where the values on the wall do not match the behaviors in the room.

At the same time, diversity is the key to innovation. Study after study confirms this. A 2020 report by Boston Consulting Group found that companies with more diverse management teams generated 19 percent higher innovation revenue than those with less diverse leadership. That is not just a social win. That is a business one. The very differences that make collaboration more complex also make creativity more powerful. Diverse teams see what others miss. They challenge assumptions. They widen the lens.

But they also slow down trust. They take longer to build cohesion. Because difference, by definition, creates distance that must be intentionally bridged. That bridge takes leadership, not luck. It takes skill, not slogans.

And without that skill, without that structure, the very thing that promises to move an organization forward can feel like it is pulling it apart.

That is the unspoken fear in many leadership rooms. It is not always that people are against diversity. It is that they are unsure whether their culture is strong enough to hold it. Because without clarity, without intention, without the courage to manage the tension that difference brings, diversity will threaten the cohesion that culture requires to survive.

This is why many cultures retreat from diversity the moment it becomes real. Not because they do not value difference, but because they never built the scaffolding to hold it.

And yet this is exactly where the opportunity lies. The strongest cultures of the future will not be the most aligned or the most comfortable. They will be the ones with the capacity to hold tension without collapsing. The ones that know who they are and still make room for who they are becoming.

Not every culture is ready for diversity. But those that are willing to do the hard work—of naming, designing, and leading across difference—will be the ones that build organizations that last.

Why Some Want Diversity and Others Don't

The conversation about diversity in the United States is rarely about the words we use. It is about what those words represent. For some, diversity is a business imperative. It is a growth strategy that allows organizations to better understand markets, connect with customers, and compete in a world that is only becoming more global and complex. In these environments, diversity is not just a value. It is a tool. It is smart business.

For others, diversity feels like a political liability. It is seen not as an asset, but as an accusation. It conjures fears of being left behind, talked down to, or forced to accommodate identities they do not understand. In these cases, diversity is framed as a threat, not because it is inherently dangerous, but because it represents a shift in control.

There are also those who approach diversity through the lens of justice. For them, it is about righting wrongs, correcting structural inequities, and restoring dignity to those who have been historically excluded. Diversity is not optional in this view. It is a moral obligation.

And then there are those for whom diversity signals erosion. It becomes a symbol of lost identity, of diluted values, of unfamiliar norms taking over familiar space. These are not always the loudest voices in the room. But they are often the most resistant. Not out of hatred, but out of fear.

This is not just about ideology. This is about identity. Leaders and communities interpret diversity through their own histories and fears. Through their sense of safety. Through their definitions of success. Until we are willing to address the motivations beneath these responses, we will keep designing strategies that fail. We will keep creating language that people do not trust. We will keep offering programs that people quietly resent.

You cannot impose a cultural shift on people who have not been given the space to process what that shift costs them. And yet, this is what many organizations continue to do. They treat diversity as a blanket policy, applied equally across all people and places, assuming that agreement will follow structure.

But agreement does not come from structure. It comes from meaning. It comes from resonance. And that is what we must start building.

A Future Lens: What Diversity Will and Should Become

It is time to stop pretending that one version of diversity can work everywhere. What we need now is not uniformity. We need a framework that is lens-based. One that understands context, nuance, and culture. Diversity must be translated and then implemented.

In some environments, diversity will need to prioritize experience and economic class. In others, it will need to center neurodiversity, spiritual identity, or political ideology. This is not dilution. This is design. It is a move away from universal definitions and toward adaptive application. We are not abandoning shared values. We are shaping them with precision. That is what maturity looks like. That is what sustainable leadership requires.

If we want diversity to survive this cultural moment, we have to stop forcing it into one narrative. We must let it become what it was always meant to be: a container that holds complexity, not a campaign that erases it.

Diversity in Different Contexts: Different Motives. Different Implications.

The biggest cultural misstep of the last decade has been the assumption that diversity means the same thing to everyone. It does not. In fact, diversity has never meant the same thing across sectors or communities. What we have done is use the same word across every environment without first addressing the motivations behind it. We have used diversity as a universal solution to very different problems. That is why the backlash was inevitable. People were responding not just to what diversity was, but to what it was being used to achieve.

We cannot move forward until we name what different groups want from diversity. Because no one wants it for the same reasons. And the reasons shape everything.

In business, the motive behind diversity has always been revenue. Corporate America talks about values, but it responds to margins. From the beginning, diversity initiatives in business were justified by how well they supported the bottom line. Whether through marketing strategies aimed at customer segmentation, branding that appealed to younger generations, or internal hiring practices designed to access top talent, diversity has been positioned as a lever for growth. Companies embraced it to gain a competitive advantage.

Diversity was a way to attract new markets, understand consumer behavior, increase innovation, and build global teams that reflected global clients. It was about performance. McKinsey found that companies in the top quartile for ethnic and gender diversity were significantly more likely to outperform peers on profitability. That data matters. It always has. And that is the point. Business leaders do not invest in diversity because it is right. They invest when it works. That does not make the motive bad, but it does make it specific.

In moral frameworks, the motive is restoration. This group does not look to diversity to increase profit. It looks to diversity to repair harm. This is the language of justice, of reparative leadership, of accountability to history. In these spaces, diversity is about truth-telling, redress, and dignity. It is about calling attention to the people and communities that were intentionally excluded from access, opportunity, and safety. Whether through slavery, segregation, colonialism, or systemic bias, the goal here is not balance sheets. It is healing. It is making things right. And for that reason, moral frameworks tend to push further and harder than other groups. They do not want cosmetic change. They want structural shifts. Power shifts. Policy shifts. And those shifts are threatening to the very systems that benefit from the status quo. That is why this form of diversity is often the first to be labeled as radical or divisive. Because it demands something deeper than optics. It demands transformation.

In spiritual communities, the motive is obedience. For faith-based organizations and institutions, diversity is often approached as a reflection of divine intention. Some traditions frame it through the lens of creation, emphasizing that all people are made in the image of God and should be welcomed accordingly. Others interpret diversity as a test of discipleship—how we treat the outsider, the foreigner, the one who is different. Still others wrestle with the boundaries between inclusion and theological conviction. For these communities, diversity is not a strategy. It is a matter of faithfulness. That is why the conversation can be both profound and polarizing. It raises questions about doctrine, about purity, about authority. It is not simply about making room. It is about discerning whether that room changes who we believe we are. As the culture shifts around them, many spiritual leaders are being forced to answer a difficult question: can we make space for diversity without compromising the truth we are called to uphold? The tension here is not business risk. It is spiritual integrity. And the consequences, for many, feel eternal.

In homogeneous communities, the motive is preservation, but often it is also protection from perceived annihilation. These are environments where identity and belonging are tightly linked to sameness. Culture, values, tradition, and even opportunity have been passed down through consistency. Diversity, when introduced without context or shared vision, is not simply perceived as change. It can feel like extinction. In these communities, the fear is not just that difference will disrupt the norm. It is that difference will replace the norm. That their children will have fewer chances. That their values will no longer be respected. That the moral center of their community will be lost. These fears are not always articulated in public, but they shape private resistance and political reaction. Fear and hostility often exist side by side. In some cases, fear justifies rejection. In others, it deepens into anger. But the underlying motive is not always cruelty. Often, it is desperation to protect what feels like the last hold on meaning, safety, or opportunity. Leaders working in these communities must not rush to impose new language. They must first slow down long enough to understand the losses people are bracing for. Because when you feel like the future is being built without you, it is hard to welcome its architects.

In diverse communities, the motive is survival and self-determination. Unlike the other groups, diversity is not a theory in these spaces. It is a lived experience. It is a condition of daily life. These are environments—often urban, global, or multigenerational—where no one group holds majority influence. People learn early how to code-switch, how to navigate different cultural norms, how to share space with others who do not see the world the same way. Diversity is not something to be added. It is something to be managed. The motive here is not appearance. It is effectiveness. These communities know that leadership must reflect complexity. They know that decisions must be made with multiple voices in the room. And they are already modeling the future that others are still trying to imagine. What they need is not permission to lead. What they need is investment, support, and recognition. Because the tools of tomorrow are already being practiced in these spaces today.

A 2023 Pew Research study found that while 65 percent of Americans believe diversity makes the country stronger, only 24 percent say their communities are actually very diverse. That gap is not just demographic. It is motivational. It reveals a country where people are open to the idea of diversity but unsure of its relevance to their actual lives.

And that is where the work must begin. We cannot lead people into diversity if we do not first understand what they want from it. Until we speak to motive, we will keep misapplying the message. Diversity is not dead. But it is demanding something far more honest than we have given it before.

Delivering on Diversity: What It Will Take From Each Context

If diversity is going to survive in the United States, it will not be because we all agreed on the same definition. It will be because we finally understood that different groups are called to deliver it differently. Each group—business, moral frameworks, spiritual institutions, homogeneous communities, and diverse communities—has something unique to gain from doing diversity well. Not just something to offer, but something to become.

Diversity will not thrive through imitation. It will thrive through alignment.

For business, diversity will future-proof the brand by aligning it with the customer.

In a world where consumers are more diverse, more values-conscious, and more digitally connected than ever, businesses that reflect the complexity of their customers will win. Diversity enables companies to listen better, design smarter, and market more authentically. It strengthens the ability to attract, serve, and retain diverse customers whose expectations are shaped by culture, identity, and lived experience. This is not only a moral imperative. It is a market one. Companies that understand this will stop chasing representation as a trend and start embedding it as a core business function. Diversity protects against cultural missteps, builds brand loyalty, and unlocks growth in untapped segments. Internally, it produces stronger teams, broader thinking, and deeper innovation. Companies that take diversity seriously will not just grow. They will become more human, more responsive, and more connected to the people they exist to serve. They will not just compete in the market. They will reflect it.

For moral frameworks, diversity will protect long-term credibility and deepen cultural relevance.

Movements that speak of justice must reflect justice. When diversity is delivered through repair and accountability, it protects the integrity of the mission. It gives substance to the claim that equity matters. For these institutions, diversity is not a distraction. It is the embodiment of what they already stand for. It ensures that internal decisions match external advocacy. It builds cultural memory into the system. When it is done with clarity and humility, it becomes a source of trust. Diversity, embraced honestly, allows moral frameworks to walk their talk and to remain credible across generations.

For spiritual communities, diversity will reawaken purpose and re-establish trust.

People are leaving faith institutions not because they do not believe in God, but because they no longer see the institution living out the message. Diversity, embraced through spiritual conviction rather than cultural guilt, allows these communities to return to their roots. It is not about abandoning truth. It is about embodying it more fully. A community that can honor difference while remaining anchored in faith becomes a sanctuary in the truest sense of the word. The world is desperate to see unity without uniformity. Faith communities are uniquely positioned to show what that looks like. Diversity will restore the relevance of spiritual spaces when they lead with obedience rather than appearance.

For homogeneous communities, diversity will challenge comfort but build capacity.

These communities will not experience diversity as validation. They will experience it as disruption. But that disruption is where strength is built. Diversity, when engaged intentionally, will expand cultural intelligence, spark creativity, and build adaptive muscle. It will challenge assumptions and create new ways of thinking. It will not always feel safe, but it will lead to growth. And in that growth, these communities will become more resilient in the face of change, more capable of cross-boundary leadership, and more confident in their ability to shape the future rather than fear it. Diversity will not erase who they are. It will stretch who they are into something more equipped. In doing so, it will also increase agency, the power to act with purpose and vision in a changing world.

For diverse communities, diversity will unlock greater capacity to lead, contribute, and influence.

These communities have carried the complexity of difference for generations. They know how to navigate identity, power, and pluralism because they have had to. With intentional support, they can move from managing diversity to leveraging it. They will not only model new systems. They will drive them. Diversity will become a source of leadership, not just survival. These communities will shape the economy, transform civic life, and build innovations that benefit society as a whole. Their capacity to contribute to business, to culture, policy, and to education will be fully visible. No longer asked to prove themselves, they will be positioned to lead.

Diversity will not give the same return to every group. But it will give each group what it most needs to evolve. For business, relevance. For justice communities, integrity. For faith communities, renewal. For homogeneous communities, strength and agency. For diverse communities, power and platform.

That is why diversity must be delivered differently. That is why it must be designed through the lens of each community's truth. The future of diversity will not be built on declarations. It will be built on design.

The Danger of Uncertainty: When Culture Is Weak, Diversity Feels Threatening

Weak cultures adopt values they cannot support. They say all the right things, but lack the structure, clarity, and leadership to live them out. The mission is fuzzy. The behaviors are inconsistent. The language is aspirational but ungrounded. And when that is the case, diversity does not feel like progress. It feels like chaos.

That is when backlash takes hold. Sometimes it comes loudly. Other times it shows up in silence, slow attrition, or quiet resistance. People do not reject diversity itself. They reject what it reveals. Diversity exposes confusion, contradiction, and unresolved tensions. When culture is uncertain, differences becomes destabilizing.

Diversity needs spine. It must be held up by clear answers to critical questions. Who are we? Who belongs here? What are we building together? When those answers are solid, diversity becomes a source of strength. When those answers are missing, diversity becomes the lightning rod for every discomfort and every fear.

Without anchor points, difference does not produce creativity. It produces confusion. It does not deepen insight. It multiplies suspicion. What we often call culture wars are not just ideological clashes. They are symptoms of shallow cultures that have not done the work of defining who they are.

Strong cultures are not threatened by diversity because they are grounded. They are not trying to please everyone. They are trying to build something with the right people. They know what they believe. They know how they make decisions. They know what is non-negotiable and what can stretch. That clarity makes space for difference. Not just safe space, but shared space with purpose.

When leaders are unclear, culture stays uncertain. And when culture is uncertain, diversity will always feel like too much. Not because it is. But because the organization has not yet built the strength to hold what it claims to value.

Courage over Comfort: Naming What You Actually Believe

This moment is not calling for compliance. It is calling for courage. The kind of leadership that does not rely on borrowed language or polished statements, but on conviction. The kind that does not just follow trends, but names truth.

Leaders are being asked to move beyond policy into philosophy. Not just what you allow, but what you stand for. Not just what you permit, but what you protect.

Do you actually believe that diversity improves performance? Do you believe that bringing in people with different backgrounds, experiences, and perspectives leads to better outcomes. Or have you said it so many times that you stopped checking whether you meant it.

Are you willing to include people whose values challenge yours? Not just people who look different, but people who think differently. People who may ask questions you would rather avoid. People who may not fit the profile of comfort but might bring the insight you need.

Will you prioritize representation when it costs you comfort. When it slows down consensus. When it requires explaining yourself again. When it means letting go of control. Or will your commitment to diversity disappear the moment it disrupts your rhythm?

These are not surface-level questions. These are identity-level questions. They are about who you are as a leader and what kind of culture you are willing to build.

Culture is not shaped by what you write in a handbook. It is shaped by what you protect when no one is watching. It is shaped by whose voice you defend. Whose presence you normalize. Whose leadership you elevate. And whose difference you refuse to manage away.

Comfort will keep you predictable. Courage will make you real. And right now, only one of those will move your organization forward.

The End of Performative Diversity. The Rise of Designed Culture.

We are witnessing the collapse of surface-level inclusion. The kind that was built to be seen more than felt. The kind that lived in headlines, metrics, and glossy reports, but never quite made it into decision-making, power-sharing, or truth-telling. That version of diversity is not evolving. It is ending.

Diversity is not dying. It is shedding its costume. It is removing the layers of language, branding, and performance that once made it popular but never made it powerful. What is emerging in its place is something leaner, stronger, and far more demanding. Not a campaign. A commitment. Not an initiative. A design.

The next era will not reward optics. It will reward alignment. Alignment between what is said and what is done. Between what is valued and what is funded. Between whom is included and who is heard. It will be less about who is on the website and more about who is in the room when the stakes are high.

This shift will require a new kind of leader. Someone who understands that culture is not just about cohesion. It is also about expansion. Real culture does not remain safe by staying small. It becomes strong by stretching wisely. Leaders who can design cultures that hold clarity and complexity at the same time will be the ones who thrive in what is coming next.

Performative diversity is easy to applaud but impossible to sustain. Designed culture is slower, harder, and far more honest. It makes space for difference without losing direction. It builds systems that are both rooted and responsive.

That is what the moment is calling for now. Not another statement. Not another committee. But a deeper commitment to culture as the operating system of everything. Diversity will survive. But only if it is built into that system on purpose.

Summary: The Beauty and the Burden

Diversity is both gift and grind. At its best, it expands imagination, unlocks innovation, and widens the circle of who gets to belong. It helps organizations see customers more clearly, solve problems more creatively, and tell a truer story about who they serve. That beauty is real, and in many markets it becomes a competitive advantage that compounds over time.

The challenge is just as real. Diversity slows familiar rhythms, exposes fragile norms, and demands new competencies that not every organization has or wants to build. Some leaders will opt in by conviction. Others will opt out by limitation. Both choices carry consequences. Opting in without design creates chaos. Opting out without honesty creates cynicism. Only those who pair conviction with capability will see durable returns.

The truth is balanced. Diversity will not save a weak culture, but a clear and strong culture can hold diversity without losing its center. It will not be the right path for everyone, and not everyone will choose it. For those who do, and who build the skill to lead across difference with clarity, equity, and inclusion, diversity will be more than a statement. It will be a strategic advantage, a moral witness, and a human good.

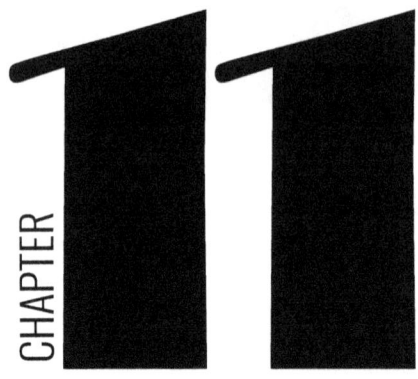

CHAPTER 11

FUTURE STATE OF WORK AND IMPACT ON CULTURE

We were halfway through building a strategic plan when the executive team hit pause. Not because they didn't agree on the goals, but because they weren't sure what they were building the plan for. The usual questions—where should we invest, how do we increase efficiency, how do we upskill—were all being asked through a lens that no longer worked. One leader finally voiced what everyone else was circling around:

"I don't think we know what we are anymore. And I'm not just talking about the org chart."

The room went silent. Not from disagreement, but from recognition. It was a moment of cultural disorientation. AI had changed everything. The market was no longer local or even global, it was instant. Talent didn't just want flexibility; they wanted a voice. Every assumption about what made their organization strong, stable, and future-ready felt like it belonged to last year. Maybe last quarter.

They didn't need a plan. They needed clarity.

So, we scrapped the PowerPoint and started mapping instead. Not just the business strategy, but the belief system that would need to support it. The culture infrastructure underneath it. We asked two questions: What's coming? And who do we need to become to thrive in that future?

The answers weren't just about AI, or tech, or policy. They were about people. Relationships. Meaning. Boundaries. Creativity. Purpose. The future of work is not just a shift in tools, roles, or schedules. It is a full-scale Re-imagination of how culture works—and who it's actually for. That's what this chapter is about. The signals are everywhere. Some started years ago. Some exploded overnight. But they all point to one reality:

Culture must evolve—or it will erode.

Let's trace the fault lines that brought us here, and the irreversible forces reshaping the ground beneath us. Then we'll explore what leaders must prepare for, and how to build cultural clarity in a future where nothing else stays still.

The Pandemic Was the First Crumble

The coronavirus pandemic didn't just disrupt routines—it exposed the thin glue holding a lot of workplace cultures together. When the meetings stopped, when the walls disappeared, when people were left alone with their values, priorities, and children staring at them through Zoom, a quiet rebellion began. Culture used to be about presence. Now it had to be about relevance.

We saw who led with empathy and who led with fear. We saw which organizations had true clarity and which were hiding behind performance theater. The pandemic wasn't just a health crisis—it was a cultural x-ray.

And it revealed something hard: most cultures weren't built to flex.

For Baby Boomers, the pandemic forced a confrontation with the meaning of loyalty. For Gen X leaders, it tested whether stability could survive under disruption. Millennials used it to demand boundaries and meaning. Gen Z entered the workforce with the assumption that flexibility wasn't a perk—it was the baseline. Leaders can't forget: those generational imprints didn't vanish when offices reopened. They hardened into expectations.

Then Came AI—And It Didn't Ask Permission

Generative AI didn't knock. It barged in. Suddenly creativity wasn't just human. ChatGPT wrote memos. Midjourney designed logos. AI assistants started scheduling, writing, and thinking. The knee-jerk reaction was fear. But deeper than fear was confusion. What does culture mean in a world where your teammate might be a machine? Here's the twist: AI didn't destroy human value. It spotlighted it. The more machines think, the more human connection matters. The more creativity is outsourced, the more originality matters. The more predictable AI becomes, the more relationships become the differentiator.

AI pushed us to ask: If intelligence is no longer our advantage, what is? The answer: trust, meaning, love, spirit, intuition. Not soft stuff. Strategic stuff.

For younger generations who grew up with AI in their hands, it's a tool. For older generations, it's a disruption. Leaders must hold the tension: integrating AI without erasing the human center.

And Then the Diversity Lie Collapsed

Somewhere in the pursuit of representation, we started equating culture with diversity. But let's be honest. Diversity is only a strength when it's integrated. Most organizations didn't build culture with diversity at the foundation. They built culture and tried to layer diversity on top—like sprinkles on concrete.

But culture is about shared meaning, not surface-level variation. Real diversity—of thought, background, and values—requires real courage. Because the opposite of a strong culture isn't uniformity. It's uncertainty. Performative inclusion gave way to silent resentment. Brave voices were asked to quiet down for harmony. And people stopped trusting cultures that couldn't define what they were protecting.

Leaders must now recognize for some, diversity is a moral imperative. For others, it's a business strategy. And for still others, it's optional—or even a distraction. Generations split here, too: younger employees often demand visible alignment, while older ones may expect neutrality or silence. A strong culture doesn't avoid the tension. It names who it's for, what it stands for, and how inclusion shows up in practice.

Quantum Computing and the Collapse of Certainty

If AI shook up your workflows, quantum computing will make you question the nature of reality itself. Unlike AI, which automates, quantum accelerates—processing millions of possibilities at once instead of step by step.

Industries like finance, cybersecurity, logistics, and pharmaceuticals will leap forward. Encryption will be broken. Business models will crumble overnight. The shift won't be gradual—it will be sudden.
What does this mean for culture?

- Decision windows shrink. Cultures addicted to consensus will collapse. Trust and ethical reflexes will matter more than perfect information.
- Transparency becomes real. Privacy as we know it dissolves. Integrity will no longer be aspirational—it will be survival.
- Ethics move to the center. With exponential power, every choice carries massive consequences. Leaders will need spiritual and moral clarity, not just technical savvy.
- • Leadership shifts from control to consciousness. Boomers and Gen X may need to let go of hierarchy. Millennials and Gen Z, more fluent in fluid networks, will push for distributed wisdom.

The question is not whether quantum is coming—it is: what will it expose in you?

The Gig Economy and Flex Workforces: Loyalty Has Left the Building

The gig economy is no longer a side hustle. It's the economy. Freelancers, contractors, consultants, nearly half the workforce now identifies as flexible.

But here's the rub: many of them don't want to be part of your culture. They want to be respected by it, aligned with it, maybe influenced by it—but not owned by it.

For older generations raised on tenure, this feels like betrayal. For Millennials and Gen Z, it's freedom.

Leaders must respond by:

- Building cultures that are modular, not monolithic.
- Shifting loyalty from tenure to alignment.
- Designing onboarding as a covenant, not an assimilation.

No one owes you their loyalty. You must earn their alignment—daily.

Hybrid and Global Work Environments: Culture Without Borders—or Walls

Hybrid isn't new, but globalization has made it unavoidable. Teams span continents, cultures, and time zones. This isn't the exception. It's Tuesday.

The old assumption—that proximity creates connection—is gone. Connection must now be designed. Leaders must treat culture as a principle, not place.

Gen Z may feel more at home building trust on a Google Doc than in a boardroom. Boomers may still expect handshakes and eye contact. Neither is wrong—but leaders must translate culture across generational and geographic lines.

If you can't explain your culture without pointing to your office walls, then your culture isn't strong. It's convenient.

Customized Benefits and the Rise of Individualized Value Exchange

Once, benefits were standardized: health, retirement, tuition. Today? They're customized. Some want fertility coverage. Others want daily pay. Others want float holidays for spiritual observances.

This isn't entitlement. It's a generational shift. Boomers built identity around security. Gen X wants balance. Millennials want flexibility and growth. Gen Z wants integration between who they are and where they work.

Leaders must stop treating benefits as compliance and start treating them as culture. Benefits are culture signals—proof of what you value.

Shortened Workdays and AI-Powered Productivity: The Time Illusion Is Over

The eight-hour day is a relic. AI has made hours irrelevant, but most organizations are still pretending.

For Boomers and Gen X, hours equaled trust. For Millennials and Gen Z, output and creativity are the real currency. Leaders must pivot now:

- Redefine performance around outcomes, not time.
- Build cultures that protect energy, not exhaust it.
- Normalize rest as strategy, not luxury.

If you cling to hours, you'll lose your best talent first.

Service Economy + High Intellects: The Death of the Middle Manager

The squeeze is in the middle. Service workers are supervised by apps. High intellect workers collaborate in flat, digital networks. The traditional middle manager—the translator of goals and the keeper of systems—is vanishing.

If you're a middle leader, your new job is not control. It's meaning-making. Coaching. Anchoring culture.

Generational divides cut here too. Younger leaders expect mentorship, not micromanagement. Older leaders may cling to hierarchy. The leaders who survive will be those who can mentor across generations—translating values into lived experience.

Segmenting Culture by Belief: The New Rules of Belonging

Culture is not neutral. It is directional. People now bring their politics, spirituality, and identity to work—and expect culture to either hold it or reject it.

Leaders can no longer pretend that "work is work." Gen Z especially demands moral clarity. Boomers may prefer neutrality. Millennials expect activism. Gen X wants balance.

You cannot satisfy everyone. But you must define your center: who you are, what you value, and how you treat people when beliefs diverge.

Inclusion without intention is chaos. Strong culture is not universal. It is clear.

The Leader's Charge: Design the Future Before It Designs You

You cannot pause the future. You can only shape it.

AI writes. Quantum thinks. Gig workers flow in and out. Global teams span continents. Middle managers vanish. Benefits fragment. Subcultures multiply.

The leaders who thrive will not be the ones with the best decks. They will be the ones with the most clarity.

Clarity about what they protect.
Clarity about who they are built for.

Clarity about what they will not compromise.
This is not HR strategy. It is spiritual discipline.

The future will not wait. The only question is whether your culture rises to meet it—or becomes one more casualty of the past.

Cultural Shift

CULTURAL SHIFT	OLD MODEL	EMERGING MODEL	LEADERSHIP RESPONSE
Quantum Computing	Decision-making with time and hierarchy	Instant decisions, multi-dimensional data	Build deep trust, train ethical reflexes, lead with wisdom not speed
Gig Economy + Flex Workforces	Loyalty based on tenure and job title	Alignment based on values and opportunity	Create flexible cultural contracts, earn alignment daily
Hybrid + Global Work	Culture shaped by physical presence	Culture shaped by digital rhythm and clarity	Lead asynchronously, honor localization, define values that travel
Customized Benefits	One-size-fits-all perks and policies	Individualized value exchange and co-creation	Signal values through benefits, offer relevance not just fairness
Shortened Workdays + AI Productivity	Hours = output, managers track time	Outcomes = value, AI supports focus	Redefine performance, protect energy, prioritize creativity
Service Economy + High Intellects	Middle managers enforce systems	Middle disappears, replaced by self-led teams	Elevate mid-level leaders into mentors, connectors, cultural anchors
Subcultures + Fragmentation	Culture as universal, generic inclusion	Culture segmented by belief, value, and purpose	Name your center, lead with conviction, include with clarity

The future of work is not a single shift. It is the collision of many: pandemics that shattered presence, AI that redefined intelligence, diversity debates that exposed uncertainty, quantum computing that will collapse time, gig work that erases loyalty, hybrid models that dissolve borders, and generational divides that sharpen expectations.

Chapter after chapter, we've traced how each of these forces exposed culture's fractures—and revealed culture's strength. Now, in the future state of work, they converge.

What leaders need most is not more slogans or strategies, but cultural strength that can flex and hold at the same time. And that is where we go next. From philosophy to practice. From description to measurement. From the poetry of culture to the math that makes it replicable.

CHAPTER 12

DEFINING & OPERATIONALIZING CULTURE STRENGTH

I was sitting with a CEO who looked at me with great confidence and said, "Our culture is strong. People stay here for decades. Turnover is almost nonexistent." He leaned back as if the case was closed. But when I asked what kind of culture they had intentionally built, he went quiet. After a pause, he admitted they didn't really have a defined model—they were simply proud that people didn't leave.

The board loved those numbers. Stability looked like strength on paper. But when I met with mid-level managers, I heard a different truth. Employees stayed because it felt risky to leave, not because the culture inspired them to stay. They had built a culture of fear disguised as loyalty.

That conversation taught me something I've carried into every client engagement since. Culture strength is not about whether it looks impressive from the outside. It is about whether the culture you've intentionally defined is the culture people actually live every day. Without a model, without a vision, you're not measuring strength. You're only measuring shadows.

The mistake leaders often make is assuming culture is normative, that strength means one-size-fits-all: innovative like a tech company, customer-obsessed like a retailer, or mission-driven like a nonprofit. But the real measure of strength is not whether your culture looks like someone else's, it is whether it looks like yours.

Why Culture Needs Technical Rigor

That CEO's pause is the reason culture work too often collapses under its own weight. Leaders are comfortable saying they want a "great culture," but very few are comfortable treating culture with the same rigor they treat strategy, finance, or operations. They call it "soft stuff" as if softness makes it secondary. Yet the truth is simple: culture is as hard-edged as revenue. It either drives it or drains it.

Strong cultures are not accidents, and they are not slogans. They are systems. They are built with the same intentionality as a product launch or a capital investment. If you cannot define the model, you cannot measure it. If you cannot measure it, you cannot operationalize it. And if you cannot operationalize it, you will not sustain it.

This is where leaders stumble. They fall in love with another organization's mythology. They borrow Netflix's rules of freedom, Google's story of innovation, or Chick-fil-A's values of service. But borrowed culture is like borrowed shoes: they may shine for a moment, but they will never fit.

The truth is, culture is not normative. There is no single right version. A culture of high precision can be as strong as a culture of rapid experimentation. A culture of stability can be as strong as a culture of disruption. What matters is not the content of the culture, but the congruence between what you say you want and what people experience every day.

That is where technical rigor comes in. When you treat culture like a strategic asset—one that can be designed, measured, tracked, and held accountable—you move it out of the realm of aspiration and into the realm of execution. Boards stop asking "do we have a good culture?" and start asking "is our culture strong against the model we defined?" That is the shift from vague pride to operational clarity.

Defining Culture Strength in Operational Terms

Before you can measure strength, you must define what strong means for you. This is where most organizations skip a step. They jump into engagement surveys, benchmarking reports, or best-practice case studies without first declaring the culture they are actually trying to build. That is like hiring a personal trainer and never saying whether your goal is to run a marathon, increase flexibility, or lose weight. You cannot measure progress against an undefined destination.

Your culture model or vision is that destination. It is not a list of generic values printed on the wall, it is a clear picture of what you want your culture to look like, feel like, and sound like inside your organization.

I often push executives with questions like:

- What would someone new notice in their first 90 days here?
- If your culture disappeared tomorrow, what behaviors, rituals, or attitudes would you fight to protect?
- What is the most important way you want your organization to be different from others in your industry?

The answers reveal the beginnings of a culture model. Some leaders will emphasize customer obsession. Others will prioritize precision, stability, or risk-taking. Some will elevate social responsibility or inclusiveness. There is no universal hierarchy of values. The point is not to choose what is most fashionable, but to name what is most authentic to your mission.

Once the culture model is articulated, it becomes the benchmark. Every measure of culture strength must be tied back to it. If innovation is core to your model, then the relevant metrics might include the number of new ideas implemented, or the percentage of revenue from products less than two years old. If equity and fairness are core, then promotion patterns and pay equity become primary measures. If speed is essential, then decision velocity and cycle times are the right indicators.

Culture strength, then, is best defined as the degree of alignment and reinforcement between the model you have declared and the reality people live every day. That alignment shows up in three domains:

- Systems: Are policies, performance processes, and governance designed to reinforce the culture model?
- Symbols: Do your stories, rituals, recognition programs, and physical spaces embody it?
- Behaviors: Do leaders and employees consistently act in ways that reflect it?

When the model is clear and these three domains reinforce it, culture strength emerges. When the model is fuzzy or the domains are inconsistent, culture weakness creeps in.

This is the pivot from aspiration to accountability. Without a model, every measurement is noise. With a model, every measurement has meaning.

Key Dimensions and Indicators of Culture Strength

Once an organization has defined its culture model, the next step is translating that vision into dimensions that can be tracked. Otherwise, "culture" remains a story people tell instead of a system leaders manage.

Every culture will have its own priorities, but there are core dimensions that almost always reveal whether a culture is strong or fragile. Think of them as lenses through which you can test the alignment between your declared model and lived reality.

Clarity of Values

- Do employees know the organization's values without a poster in front of them?
- Indicator: percentage of employees who can name the top three values unprompted.
- Indicator: percentage of leaders who can explain how those values inform decision-making.

Behavioral Consistency

- Do leaders behave in ways that reinforce the stated model?
- Indicator: results of 360-degree feedback tied to organizational values.
- Indicator: percentage of employees who agree their leaders "practice what they preach."

Decision Velocity

- Does the culture accelerate or slow decision-making?
- Indicator: average time-to-decision at executive and manager levels.
- Indicator: ratio of decisions made at the right level (not pushed unnecessarily upward).

Engagement and Retention

- Are people choosing to give discretionary effort, loyalty, and advocacy because of the culture?
- Indicator: employee engagement survey results segmented by alignment questions ("I feel our culture supports me in doing my best work").
- Indicator: regrettable turnover rate vs. industry benchmark.
- Indicator: employee Net Promoter Score (eNPS).

Adaptability

- Can the culture flex without losing its core identity?
- Indicator: success rate of major change initiatives (measured against milestones).
- Indicator: percentage of employees who report confidence in adapting to change.
- Indicator: speed of integration in mergers or restructuring.

Integrity of Alignment

- Is there congruence between what is said and what is lived?
- Indicator: gap between "espoused values" (on paper) and "experienced values" (survey, interviews, ethnographic observation).
- Indicator: frequency of compliance or ethics violations tied to values lapses.

Notice something important: these are not normative measures. They are not designed to say one culture is better than another. They are designed to say whether your culture is strong against the model you defined.

For example, a financial institution that values risk management may consider "slow, deliberate decisions" a positive indicator of strength, while a tech startup may consider "rapid experimentation" the very measure of strength. The difference is not in which is stronger, but in whether each is consistent with its declared culture model.

The key is that strength shows up in **alignment and reinforcement across clarity, consistency, speed, engagement, adaptability, and integrity.** These dimensions create a technical architecture for measuring culture that leaders can actually manage.

Methods to Measure Culture Strength

Once the dimensions are clear, the next challenge is measurement. Leaders often default to engagement surveys, but those only scratch the surface. To truly measure culture strength, you need a portfolio of methods, quantitative and qualitative, that capture alignment across systems, symbols, and behaviors.

Employee Surveys

Surveys remain useful, but only if they are designed to test alignment to the culture model, not just general satisfaction.

- Ask: "Do you see our values lived out in your team?" rather than "Are you satisfied with leadership?"
- Use pulse surveys quarterly for agility, not just annual snapshots.
- Segment results by team, function, or geography to find pockets of strength and weakness.

360-Degree Leadership Assessments

Culture strength is often revealed in leadership behavior. If your values include collaboration, measure it directly in how leaders are perceived by peers, direct reports, and supervisors.

- Map feedback items to values and behaviors defined in your culture model.
- Aggregate results into organizational dashboards that show where leadership is aligned or misaligned.

Observation and Ethnographic Methods

Numbers alone can deceive. Sometimes the richest culture data comes from structured observation.

- Shadow employees or leaders to observe behaviors against values.
- Conduct focus groups that explore stories: "Tell me about a time when our culture showed up at its best or worst."
- Analyze rituals, meeting patterns, and physical space—what do they reinforce?

Talent Analytics

Culture strength often reveals itself in who stays, who leaves, and who rises.

- Track regrettable turnover, internal mobility, promotion equity, and exit interview themes.
- Watch for disparities: are some groups thriving while others feel excluded?

Collaboration and Productivity Analytics

With digital tools, we can now analyze how people actually work.

- Email, calendar, and messaging data can reveal whether teams are overburdened or siloed.
- Meeting load, response times, and cross-functional communication can serve as cultural signals of efficiency, inclusivity, or bottlenecking.

Real-Time Feedback Channels

Culture can no longer wait a year to be measured.

- Build anonymous digital channels where employees can report cultural friction.
- Use quick "pulse polls" during town halls or leadership meetings to check alignment in real time.
- Treat feedback loops like oxygen for cultural clarity.

External Reputation Signals

Culture isn't only what employees experience, it's also how customers, partners, and potential recruits perceive you.

- Track employer brand ratings, Glassdoor reviews, and social sentiment.
- Compare how external narratives align, or clash, with your internal model.

When leaders combine these methods, they move beyond "gut feel" and anecdote. They create a reliable, multi-source picture of culture strength. This portfolio of measures allows them to see not just whether employees are happy, but whether the culture they have intentionally designed is truly alive.

Operationalizing Culture Strength into Daily Practice

Measurement is only half the equation. A strong culture is not a survey result or a dashboard; it is what people experience every time they interact with your organization. To operationalize culture strength, leaders must translate their defined model into daily systems, processes, and rituals that make the culture unavoidable.

Translate Values into Behaviors

Values by themselves are too abstract. To become operational, they must be defined in observable, repeatable actions.

- If a value is integrity, the behavior might be "we disclose risks early, even when it is uncomfortable."
- If a value is innovation, the behavior might be "we test ideas quickly and accept failure as part of progress."
- Build behavioral standards into job descriptions, performance reviews, and recognition programs.

Integrate Culture into Talent Processes

People practices are the most powerful levers for operationalizing culture.

- Hiring: Use interview guides tied to cultural behaviors, not just technical skills.
- Onboarding: Make the culture model the centerpiece of how people are welcomed.
- Performance Reviews: Balance results with behaviors, did this leader hit their numbers and live the culture?
- Leadership Development: Train leaders not just in skills but in how to embody and reinforce the culture.

Design Rituals and Rhythms

Culture is sustained through the small, consistent practices that shape identity.

- Daily huddles, weekly recognition moments, or storytelling at all-hands meetings can reinforce the model.
- Rituals do not have to be flashy; they simply have to be consistent and intentional.
- For example, one client made "culture moments" a standing agenda item in leadership meetings, every leader shared one recent story of the culture in action.

Embed Culture into Decision-Making

If culture is truly operational, it shapes not just how people behave, but how the organization makes decisions.

- Define decision rights in ways that reflect the culture. In a culture that values empowerment, decisions are pushed closer to the front line.
- Create "culture filters" for major initiatives: Does this choice align with our defined model? Will it reinforce or erode the culture we say we value?

Establish Governance and Accountability

Operationalizing culture requires governance, just like strategy or finance.

- Create a culture council or committee that includes leaders from across the organization.
- Review culture metrics at the executive team and board level quarterly.
- Hold leaders accountable for cultural outcomes, not just financial ones.

Connect Systems, Symbols, and Behaviors

When culture is embedded in systems (policies and processes), symbols (stories, rituals, recognition), and behaviors (leader and employee actions), it becomes self-reinforcing. Each element strengthens the others.

- Example: A company that values transparency may have open financial dashboards (system), leadership Q&A forums (symbol), and leaders who regularly admit mistakes (behavior).

The point is not perfection but consistency. When employees see the culture model reinforced in multiple ways, how they are hired, how their leaders act, how decisions are made, and how success is celebrated, they stop questioning whether the culture is real. They start living it.

Culture Dashboards and Scorecards

Too many leaders make a fatal mistake. They confuse employee engagement with culture. Engagement is whether employees feel motivated, satisfied, or proud. Culture is whether the organization consistently lives the model it claims to value. The two overlap, but they are not the same. You can have high engagement and a weak culture. You can also have a strong culture and lower engagement during seasons of stretch or crisis.

Treating engagement as culture is like mistaking a fever for the disease. Engagement is a signal, but it does not tell you whether the cultural system itself is aligned and strong.

That is why culture requires a dashboard. A dashboard is not a cosmetic exercise. It is the discipline of making the invisible visible, turning values into measurable outcomes that can be tracked, debated, and governed with the same seriousness as revenue or safety.

A culture dashboard or scorecard begins with your own model. The measures are not one-size-fits-all. They must reflect what strength looks like for your unique design. For some organizations, strength means speed and innovation. For others, it means stability and control. For still others, it means fairness and equity. The dashboard brings these priorities into quantifiable focus.

Common Culture Metrics

- Percentage of employees who can name core values unprompted
- Percentage of leaders rated "values-aligned" in 360 assessments
- Employee Net Promoter Score, measuring advocacy, not just satisfaction
- Regrettable turnover, measured against industry benchmarks
- Decision velocity, tracked by average time to major decisions
- Speed of integration during change initiatives, such as M&A or restructuring
- Equity indicators, such as promotion and pay distribution across demographics
- Culture alignment score from surveys that explicitly test behaviors against values

Turning Metrics Into a Culture Strength Index

Many organizations choose to combine several of these measures into a Culture Strength Index. The index is not meant to be perfect. It is meant to be directional, a composite signal of whether the culture you have defined is actually being lived. Just as financial indices aggregate multiple economic signals, a culture index provides a single view that executives and boards can track quarter by quarter.

Reporting and Accountability

Dashboards only matter if they are used with discipline.

- Culture results should be reviewed by the executive team and reported to the board, not just buried in HR reports
- Leader evaluations and incentives should reflect cultural outcomes as well as financial ones, otherwise culture is performative lip service
- Dashboards should be transparent enough that employees can see progress. Culture that is measured in secret erodes trust

Here is the provocation: If culture is only measured through engagement, you are not measuring culture at all. You are measuring mood. You are asking if people feel good, not if the organization is being true to itself. Mood matters, but strength matters more. Mood can rise and fall with external circumstances, but culture strength is about congruence, clarity, and resilience.

When culture becomes visible in dashboards, it stops being mythology. It becomes a managed asset. Boards stop asking, "Do we have a good culture?" and start asking, "Is our culture strong against the model we declared?" That is the shift from vanity metrics to operational truth.

Sustaining Culture Strength in Dynamic Environments

A culture that is only strong when the seas are calm is not strong at all. True strength shows itself during growth, crisis, leadership turnover, or external shock. If your culture collapses the moment conditions change, what you had was not strength but comfort.

This is why sustaining culture strength requires deliberate safeguards and early warning systems. The goal is not to freeze culture in time. The goal is to preserve its identity while allowing it to flex and adapt.

Quarterly Culture Health Reviews

Just as you would never wait a full year to review financial performance, you cannot afford to wait to review culture. Quarterly reviews of culture metrics keep leaders accountable and allow for course corrections before problems metastasize.

Early Warning Indicators

Dashboards should be designed to detect signals of fragility. Examples include:

- Unexplained spikes in regrettable turnover
- A sudden drop in "values lived" survey items even while engagement holds steady
- Increases in compliance issues or ethics violations
- Longer decision cycles in areas that previously moved quickly

These are not random blips. They are stress fractures in the cultural system.

Linking Culture Data to Business Outcomes

Boards and executives take culture seriously when it is linked to performance. Culture dashboards should correlate directly with key outcomes such as customer satisfaction, safety incidents, product innovation, and revenue growth. When leaders can see that culture is a leading indicator of financial outcomes, they stop treating it as decoration.

Resilience Mechanisms

Strong cultures do not resist change, they metabolize it. Sustaining strength requires resilience mechanisms:

- Clear rituals that remind people who they are during transition
- Communication rhythms that anchor trust when information is incomplete
- Culture champions or ambassadors in every unit who reinforce values under pressure
- Explicit onboarding for new leaders so they adopt the culture model, rather than bending it to their personal style

Guardrails During Leadership Transitions

Perhaps the greatest test of culture strength is a leadership change. Without safeguards, a new CEO or executive team can unintentionally erode culture in months. Guardrails such as onboarding into the culture model, culture immersion sessions, and transparent employee forums prevent erosion and sustain identity through change.

The Provocation

If your culture cannot survive turbulence, it was never strong. Strength is not the absence of disruption. Strength is the ability to bend without breaking. If leaders only measure culture in stable times, they are indulging in fantasy. Sustaining culture requires constant vigilance, transparent metrics, and explicit rituals that hold the organization steady even when the ground shifts.

The Practical Leader Playbook

At the end of the day, culture strength cannot be delegated. It is not an HR project, a survey, or a communications campaign. It is a leadership responsibility. The question is not whether culture exists, but whether you as a leader are actively governing it. This playbook is designed to give leaders concrete handles to do just that.

Quarterly Questions for Leaders

Every 90 days, executives should ask themselves:

- Do we have a clearly articulated culture model that is visible and understood?
- Are our systems, symbols, and behaviors reinforcing the model, or are they contradicting it?
- What are the early warning signals on our dashboard, and are we acting on them?
- Are we rewarding leaders for cultural alignment as much as for financial performance?
- Are we linking culture outcomes to business outcomes in ways the board respects?
- Are there areas of fragility where our culture could collapse under pressure?
- If a new leader joined tomorrow, would they know how to lead inside our model?

Leadership Practices That Operationalize Strength

- Review the culture dashboard alongside financial and operational metrics in executive meetings
- Make culture outcomes part of leader evaluations and compensation
- Ensure onboarding at every level includes immersion into the culture model
- Reinforce culture through rituals: storytelling, recognition, symbolic practices that tie daily work to values
- Hold open forums where employees can name when culture is aligned and when it is not

A Provocative Reminder

Culture strength is not whether people are happy. It is whether the organization is consistent, resilient, and aligned with its declared model. Leaders who confuse culture with engagement end up chasing moods. Leaders who treat culture with rigor build organizations that thrive under pressure and endure over time.

I once worked with a leadership team that, for the first time, created a culture dashboard and committed to reviewing it quarterly alongside their financials. Within six months they uncovered a troubling pattern. Turnover was low, engagement scores were stable, but values alignment was eroding in one business unit. Leaders there were hitting numbers but doing it in ways that undermined trust. Because the dashboard made it visible, they intervened early. They shifted leadership behaviors, reinforced expectations, and within a year that unit was not only hitting numbers but living the culture more authentically.

That is the difference between leading culture as a story and leading culture as a system. When you operationalize culture strength, you stop asking whether you have a good culture. You start proving, with evidence, that you have a strong one.

Summary

Chapter 11 named the forces that are reshaping work, Chapter 12 turned culture from a story into a system. We defined what strength means for you, not in slogans, but in a model you can see, measure, and run. We translated values into observable behaviors. We tied them to systems and symbols. We built dashboards that make alignment visible and hold leaders accountable. In short, we moved culture out of mythology and into management.

Now comes the choice that separates organizations that endure from those that fade. A defined model is not the finish line. It is the operating manual. Strength only lasts if you maintain it with rhythm, adapt it with wisdom, and govern it with courage. The moment you stop reviewing the signals, the drift begins. The moment you confuse engagement with culture, the erosion starts. The moment you let one leader outperform the values, the foundation cracks.

Chapter 13 is the leadership moment. It is where you decide whether culture will be actively stewarded or slowly gambled away. We will make the maintenance work explicit, the adaptation work honest, and the sustainability work non-negotiable. We will ask the questions that keep culture alive quarter after quarter, and we will set the guardrails that protect it through growth, crisis, and succession.

You built the blueprint in Chapter 12. In Chapter 13, you become its keeper.

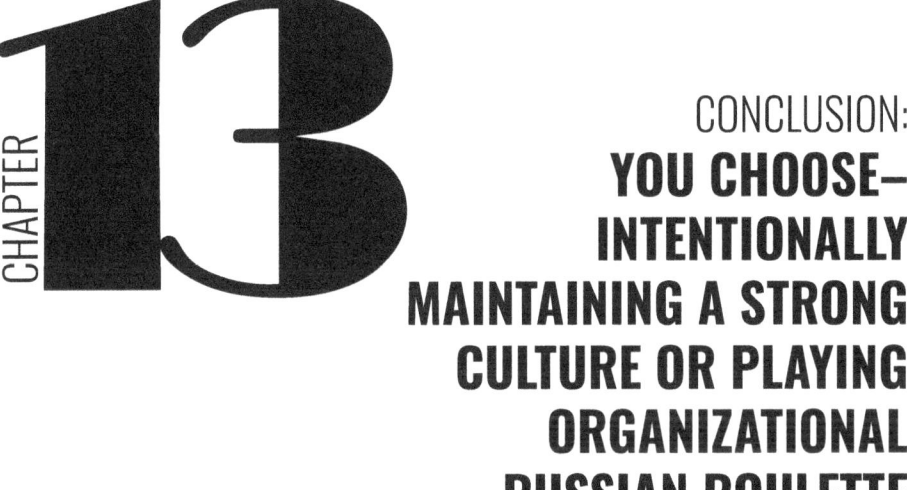

CHAPTER 13

CONCLUSION: YOU CHOOSE— INTENTIONALLY MAINTAINING A STRONG CULTURE OR PLAYING ORGANIZATIONAL RUSSIAN ROULETTE

Culture will not maintain itself. Left alone, it drifts. Left unchecked, it corrodes. Left unguarded, it collapses under pressure.

Too many leaders comfort themselves with the illusion that culture is permanent, that once declared it will carry itself forward. That is a dangerous fiction. Culture is not a slogan. It is not a speech. It is not the words etched into your headquarters wall. Culture is a living system, and like every living system it requires nourishment, care, and discipline.

This is the final truth: you must choose. You will either maintain culture intentionally, or you will gamble with it. And gambling with culture is organizational Russian Roulette. You may survive for a season, but eventually the chamber is loaded.

Maintenance is not optional

Culture maintenance is the ongoing stewardship of the environment you have built. Just as you would never assume a machine will run forever without oil or inspection, you cannot assume culture will thrive without intentional maintenance.

Strong leaders review culture as often as they review financials. They look at alignment metrics quarterly. They ask if values are visible in daily decisions, if leaders are modeling what has been declared, if systems reinforce the culture or undermine it. They do not treat culture reviews as symbolic. They treat them as operational governance.

Maintenance is not glamorous. It is the discipline of rhythm. It is the steady hand that reviews, recalibrates, and reinforces, again and again. The leaders who succeed at culture are not those who give inspiring speeches once a year. They are those who refuse to let culture slip out of sight in the ordinary grind of business.

If you are not maintaining culture, you are allowing it to decay. There is no middle ground.

Adaptation is not optional

Maintenance alone is not enough. A culture that is maintained without adaptation becomes brittle. It may be preserved, but it will not be resilient. A culture that refuses to evolve is a museum piece, admired for what it once was but incapable of leading into the future.

The world will not stop changing. Markets will shift, demographics will turn, crises will come, technologies will disrupt. If a culture does not adapt, it will eventually break.

Adaptation does not mean abandoning identity. It means holding on to the essence while evolving the expression. The strongest cultures are those that revisit their culture model periodically and ask, does this still fit who we are and where we are going. They conduct culture audits during moments of disruption. They tell new stories to make culture resonate with new generations of employees who were not there when the organization was founded.

This is not weakness. This is wisdom. Leaders who sustain culture are not sentimental. They are stewards of identity, willing to renew what must be renewed in order to protect what must endure.

If you are not refreshing culture, you are letting it fossilize.

Sustainability is not optional

Sustainability is the true test of culture strength. Any leader can generate short-term momentum. Many can build temporary engagement. But only those who nurture culture with discipline and adapt it with courage can create sustainability.

Sustainable culture is resilient enough to weather crisis, consistent enough to inspire trust, and attractive enough to retain talent for decades. It is the cultural equivalent of renewable energy, constantly replenished rather than depleted.

Without sustainability, even the best strategy is theater. A strategy may shine for a quarter, or even a few years, but without cultural sustainability the organization will eventually erode from within. Customers sense it. Employees sense it. Communities sense it. Sustainability is not about perfection. It is about creating a culture that can outlast leaders, outlast cycles, and outlast external shocks.

If you are not sustaining culture, you are presiding over its slow decline.

The false comfort of engagement

One of the greatest mistakes leaders make is confusing engagement with culture. Engagement measures mood. Culture measures identity. Engagement tells you whether people feel motivated or proud. Culture tells you whether the organization is consistent, aligned, and resilient.

It is possible to have high engagement and a weak culture. It is also possible to have strong culture and low engagement in a season of stretch. Engagement is important, but it is not the ultimate measure. Mood rises and falls with circumstance. Culture strength holds steady through turbulence.

When leaders treat engagement as culture, they chase sentiment instead of building systems. They mistake applause for alignment. They mistake smiles for strength. And they are shocked when culture collapses even though engagement surveys looked positive.

Do not confuse the two. Engagement is a signal. Culture is the system. If you chase the signal and ignore the system, you are gambling with your organization's future.

The legacy question

Every leader leaves a cultural legacy. Some leave behind drift, fragility, and confusion. Others leave behind clarity, resilience, and strength. The question is not whether you will leave a cultural legacy. The question is what kind of legacy it will be.

Financial results fade quickly. Operational wins are forgotten as the next set of challenges arrives. But culture lingers. Culture is the inheritance you pass to the people who remain after you. It shapes how they work, how they lead, how they trust, how they serve.

Ask yourself honestly: What will be remembered more about your tenure—your quarterly results, or the culture you left behind?

The final choice

This book has been about intentionality. Intentional design. Intentional leadership. Intentional culture. It ends with the starkest choice of all.

You can maintain culture intentionally. You can measure it, operationalize it, refresh it, and sustain it. You can steward it with the same rigor you bring to strategy and finance. If you do, you will leave behind an organization that is strong, resilient, and enduring.

Or you can gamble. You can treat culture as a slogan. You can assume it will take care of itself. You can confuse engagement with strength. You can comfort yourself with the illusion that stability today means sustainability tomorrow. If you do, you are spinning the chamber and hoping the trigger never pulls.

One choice secures the trust, reputation, and vitality of the organization. The other places the future at risk, even if today looks stable.

Culture always wins the long game. The only question is whether it will win for you, or against you.

The choice is yours.

APPENDICES

Appendix 1

Strong Culture Implementation Master Timeline

This timeline is designed as a project management framework for building and sustaining a strong culture. The phases are sequential, but organizations should expect iteration. Progress will include backslides and breakthroughs, and timeframes may vary by context. The goal is intentional alignment, not rigid perfection.

Phase One: Define Cultural DNA (Months 1–3)

Weeks 1–2: Stakeholder Assessment and Engagement

- Conduct executive cultural assessment and baseline analysis
- Establish a cultural steering committee with clear decision rights
- Define roles, responibilities, and reporting lines for culture governance
- Create communication frameworks to guide transparency
- Map and prioritize stakeholder groups for engagement

Weeks 3–4: Leadership Alignment

- Facilitate executive alignment workshops on cultural direction
- Secure visible leadership commitment to the transformation effort
- Develop tailored stakeholder engagement strategies by group
- Launch communication channels for open, cross-level dialogue

Weeks 5–8: Purpose, Values, and Mission Development

- Host executive working sessions to clarify identity
- Finalize purpose, vision, mission, and core values
- Align identity statements with brand, strategy, and performance expectations
- Build a cascade plan to embed understanding across the organization

Weeks 9–12: Cultural Positioning Across Dimensions

- Assess current posture across defined cultural dimensions
- Define desired cultural positioning for the future state
- Develop gap-closing strategies and micro-intervention plans
- Establish measurement criteria and accountability mechanisms

Phase Two: Build Cultural Foundation (Months 4–6)

Weeks 13–16: Rituals, Traditions, and Shared Language

- Design and pilot core rituals and meeting practices
- Identify key organizational moments to reinforce shared identity
- Introduce cultural lexicon into communications
- Document new behavioral language and train managers on usage
- Establish feedback loops to integrate employee voice

Weeks 17–20: Resource Alignment and Governance

- Review current allocation of time, talent, and budget
- Reallocate resources to strengthen cultural initiatives
- Align recognition and promotion criteria with cultural values
- Define governance structures for cultural decision-making
- Build transparent accountability and reporting systems

Weeks 21–24: Operational Reinforcement

- Audit and redesign organizational systems for cultural alignment
- Embed values into performance management and feedback cycles
- Implement reinforcement mechanisms such as dashboards and prompts
- Align decision-making and escalation processes with cultural principles

Phase Three: Sustain and Strengthen Culture (Months 7–9)

Weeks 25–28: Leadership Courage and Honesty

- Launch leadership development programs on cultural modeling
- Train leaders in authentic, values-driven communication
- Establish systems for speaking truth to power
- Build psychological safety frameworks and conflict resolution protocols
- Create supports for leaders facing cultural trade-offs

Weeks 29–32: Consistent Reinforcement Across Levels

- Integrate culture into onboarding, training, and career development
- Standardize indicators of cultural alignment across functions
- Launch coaching and mentorship networks to reinforce behaviors
- Establish peer-led reinforcement groups or cultural ambassador programs
- Create immersive cultural experiences for employees

Weeks 33–36: Recognition and Accountability Systems

- Implement recognition programs tied to cultural behaviors
- Celebrate milestones and ambassador stories across levels
- Launch accountability dashboards for culture metrics
- Conduct quarterly culture town halls and storytelling forums
- Publish leader and employee spotlights to reinforce alignment

Phase Four: Evolve and Scale Culture (Months 10–12)

Weeks 37–40: Measurement and Evaluation

- Deploy integrated cultural measurement systems
- Conduct first comprehensive cultural audit
- Host cross-level sensemaking sessions to interpret data
- Track adoption, resistance, and reinforcement behaviors
- Embed cultural KPIs into quarterly business reviews

Weeks 41–44: Adaptive Strategy Development

- Analyze data to identify friction points and hotspots
- Refine frameworks, rituals, and tools based on findings
- Support midcourse corrections and realignments
- Codify cultural methodologies into standard playbooks

Weeks 45–48: Shared Identity and Scalability

- Reinforce alignment across internal and external brand touchpoints
- Build playbooks for culture expansion into new markets or teams
- Develop adaptation guidelines for local contexts without losing identity
- Establish the shared enterprise-wide cultural story

Phase 5: Long-Term Evolution Management (Months 13–18)

Weeks 49–56: Organizational Scaling

- Expand training and cultural programs to new sites and divisions
- Adapt rituals and language by context while retaining DNA
- Launch integration strategies for global and local contexts
- Train cultural stewards to anchor values in new environments

Weeks 57–64: Cultural Evolution and Resilience

- Activate foresight and scenario planning for cultural shifts
- Create mechanisms to preserve values while adapting practices
- Engage diverse stakeholders in shaping future cultural expression
- Build organizational capacity for cultural agility

Weeks 65–72: Continuous Improvement and Innovation

- Institutionalize quarterly learning and unlearning cycles
- Build systems for culture-based innovation and idea incubation
- Launch long-term cultural effectiveness dashboards
- Refine governance to ensure agility and responsiveness
- Embed cultural insights into strategic planning cycles

Continuous Improvement Framework

Culture implementation is never finished. To sustain momentum:

- Conduct quarterly culture health reviews
- Complete annual cultural effectiveness and engagement assessments
- Keep feedback channels open across all functions and roles
- Maintain culture design and evaluation councils for ongoing oversight

Key Success Indicators

- Leadership modeling that is visible, consistent, and values-driven
- Resource allocation aligned with cultural priorities
- Consistency across language, behavior, and decision-making
- Increases in trust, discretionary effort, and advocacy
- Alignment between culture measures and core business outcomes

Critical Ongoing Actions

1. Keep leadership visible, vocal, and vulnerable
2. Communicate progress with honesty and clarity
3. Stay responsive to the culture's dynamic nature
4. Recognize and celebrate cultural champions at every level
5. Tie every cultural initiative to strategic impact

Timelines are directional, not fixed. Adjust them to context. Culture work is not linear. Expect setbacks as well as breakthroughs. The objective is not perfection but intentional alignment and continuous motion. Sustaining culture is less about repeating messages and more about translating them into daily practice.

APPENDIX 2

Cultural Implementation Troubleshooting Guide

Every cultural transformation will hit turbulence. That is not failure. That is reality. Strong cultures are not built in a straight line. They are built through iteration, tension, and course correction. The difference between organizations that thrive and those that drift is not whether challenges appear, but whether leaders face them with honesty, curiosity, and discipline.

This troubleshooting guide is written for those moments when the wheels wobble, when cultural momentum slows, or when cynicism creeps in. It offers a structured framework for diagnosis and recovery. The point is not to prevent all challenges. The point is to build resilience so challenges become catalysts rather than collapse points.

Part 1: Understanding the Issue

The instinct of most leaders is to fix quickly. Yet cultural problem-solving begins not with solutions, but with diagnosis. Think like a physician: no treatment without understanding the condition. What looks like "resistance" or "low motivation" may in fact be rational behavior inside systems that contradict stated values.

The most sophisticated organizations recognize that cultural symptoms rarely appear alone. They ripple across systems. A manufacturing company once blamed "poor employee motivation" for quality issues until they discovered their own metrics rewarded speed over accuracy. People were simply following the system that had been set for them.

Effective cultural diagnostics move in concentric circles. Start with the what—the observable manifestations. Then probe into the why—the systemic and behavioral drivers.

First-level assessment (the "what"):

Where is this happening? Who is most affected? When did it start? What metrics confirm the issue? How severe is the impact? These questions create a shared factual foundation.

Second-level investigation (the "why"):

What recent changes could have triggered ripple effects? Which systems or processes are reinforcing the wrong behaviors? What leadership signals might be contributing? What environmental pressures are shaping choices? Do employees have the skills, clarity, and resources they need? These questions reveal root causes that are often hidden in plain sight.

Part 2: Common Scenarios

Scenario 1: Leadership Inconsistency

Few things poison culture faster than leaders who say one thing but reward another. Employees notice instantly. And once trust erodes, cynicism spreads like wildfire. The most dangerous form of this is the "shadow culture"—where the official statements say one thing, but promotions, rewards, and recognition say something else. Employees will always follow the shadow.

Symptoms: mixed messages, inconsistent resource allocation, varying standards across departments, confusion about expectations, erosion of trust.

Immediate actions: document inconsistencies, convene leadership alignment sessions, clarify decision-making criteria, measure consistency, increase communication transparency.

Long-term solutions: build leadership alignment frameworks, conduct regular leadership reviews against culture, develop cultural decision-making guides, strengthen accountability systems, create strong feedback loops.

Scenario 2: Employee Resistance

Resistance is not usually stubbornness. It is often rational feedback. Employees resist when systems make adoption impossible, when incentives contradict stated priorities, or when they are being asked to change without clarity, capability, or support. Wise leaders ask what resistance is trying to tell them before labeling it a problem.

Symptoms: low participation, persistence of old behaviors, negative feedback, passive compliance, open opposition. Immediate actions: hold listening sessions, address legitimate concerns, provide support and training, create quick wins, clarify purpose and benefits.

Long-term solutions: revise change management approaches, strengthen capability training, improve engagement systems, enhance recognition, build peer support networks.

Scenario 3: System Misalignment

This is the silent killer of culture: when systems betray values. You say collaboration, but your review system ranks people against one another. You say innovation, but your budgets require twenty approvals for every new idea. Employees follow what systems reward, not what leaders say.

Symptoms: processes that conflict with values, metrics that ignore culture, recognition that celebrates the wrong behaviors, resources mis-allocated, tools that hinder alignment.

Immediate actions: identify conflicts, create workarounds, remove immediate barriers, provide extra support, communicate openly about fixes.

Long-term solutions: redesign misaligned systems, align metrics with cultural outcomes, update recognition frameworks, reallocate resources, invest in tools that reinforce desired behaviors.

Part 3: Implementation Recovery Process

Even with the best planning, culture efforts veer off course. The key is to recover quickly and deliberately.

Step 1: Pause and Assess. Gather data, listen deeply, review metrics, and document reality. Do not scramble blindly.
Step 2: Diagnose Root Causes. Go beneath surface symptoms. Map leadership behaviors, systems, employee perceptions, and external pressures.
Step 3: Design Solutions. Balance quick fixes with long-term redesign. Build support structures and define success metrics.
Step 4: Implement Changes. Start with quick wins, communicate often, monitor progress, and adjust as you go.
Step 5: Reinforce and Sustain. Celebrate progress, share learning, strengthen systems, and embed capabilities for the future.

The mark of recovery is not just correction but growth. A culture that emerges stronger, more aligned, and more resilient has turned crisis into catalyst.

Part 4: Prevention Strategies

The best troubleshooting is prevention. Strong organizations monitor culture with the same rigor they monitor revenue.

- **Cultural health monitoring**: regular pulse checks, leading indicator tracking, system alignment reviews, leadership assessments, resource adequacy reviews.

- **Early warning systems**: clear escalation paths, open feedback channels, structured stakeholder input, systematic metric monitoring.

- **Capability building**: leadership training in modeling culture, widespread change management skills, system design expertise, communication mastery, problem-solving discipline.

Proactive organizations do not eliminate challenges, but they catch cracks before they become fractures.

Part 5: Recovery Principles

Four principles should guide every recovery:

- **Transparency**: communicate honestly about what is happening, why, what to expect, and how people can help. Silence breeds rumor.

- **Learning orientation**: treat challenges as data. Every breakdown teaches something about leadership, systems, or processes.

- **Momentum building**: quick wins and visible progress matter more than grand plans in recovery. Energy rebuilds through action.

- **Support strengthening**: use recovery moments to improve infrastructure, resources, training, and networks so the next challenge is easier to withstand.

Cultural implementation challenges are not signs of failure. They are the proving ground of leadership. Each inconsistency, each pocket of resistance, each system misalignment is an invitation to lead more intentionally and build greater resilience.

Scenario	Common Symptoms	Immediate Actions	Long-Term Solutions
Leadership Inconsistency	Mixed messages about priorities, inconsistent resource allocation, standards vary across departments, employees confused about expectations, low trust in leaders	• Document inconsistencies clearly• Hold leadership alignment sessions• Clarify decision-making criteria• Establish consistency metrics• Communicate transparently	• Build leadership alignment frameworks• Conduct regular leadership reviews• Develop cultural decision-making guides• Establish accountability systems• Strengthen feedback loops
Employee Resistance	Low participation, persistence of old behaviors, negative feedback, passive compliance, open opposition	• Hold listening sessions• Address legitimate concerns• Provide support and training• Create quick wins to show progress• Clarify purpose and benefits	• Revise change management approach• Strengthen training programs• Improve engagement systems• Enhance recognition for alignment• Build peer support networks
System Misalignment	Processes contradict values, metrics ignore cultural priorities, recognition rewards wrong behaviors, resources starved, tools make aligned behaviors difficult	• Identify specific conflicts• Create temporary workarounds• Remove the biggest barriers quickly• Provide extra support• Communicate openly about fixes	• Redesign conflicting systems• Align metrics with culture outcomes• Update recognition frameworks• Reallocate resources to support culture• Invest in tools that enable alignment

REFERENCES

Chapter 1: Introduction: How to Use This Book

Citation: "Culture." Cambridge English Dictionary, Cambridge University Press, https://dictionary.cambridge.org. Accessed November 20, 2024.

Chapter 2: The Power of Culture:

How Culture Connects It All and Shapes Us

Appadurai, A. (1996). Modernity at large: Cultural dimensions of globalization. University of Minnesota Press.

Boas, F. (1940). Race, language, and culture. Macmillan.

Castells, M. (2000). The rise of the network society (2nd ed.). Blackwell.

Durkheim, E. (1912). The elementary forms of religious life. Free Press.

Geertz, C. (1973). The interpretation of cultures. Basic Books.

Hofstede, G. (1980). Culture's consequences: International differences in work-related values. Sage Publications.

Hofstede, G. (2001). Culture's consequences: Comparing values, behaviors, institutions, and organizations across nations (2nd ed.). Sage Publications.

Hofstede, G., & Bond, M. H. (1988). The Confucius connection: From cultural roots to economic growth. Organizational Dynamics, 16(4), 5–21.

Inglehart, R., & Baker, W. E. (2000). Modernization, cultural change, and the persistence of traditional values. American Sociological Review, 65(1), 19–51.

Jenkins, H. (2006). Convergence culture: Where old and new media collide. New York University Press.

Mollick, E. (2024). CoIntelligence: Living and working with AI. Portfolio.

Murphy, M. C. (2024). Cultures of growth: How the new science of mindset can transform individuals, teams and organizations. Simon & Schuster.

Nosratabadi, S., Bahrami, P., Palouzian, K., & Mosavi, A. (2020). Leader cultural intelligence and organizational performance. arXiv. https://arxiv.org/abs/2010.02678

Peters, T. J., & Waterman, R. H. (1982). In search of excellence: Lessons from America's bestrun companies. Harper & Row.

Pink, D. H. (2009). Drive: The surprising truth about what motivates us. Riverhead Books.

Ramanna, K. (2024). The age of outrage: How to lead in a polarized world. Princeton University Press.

Robinson, J., & Clegg, J. (2024). The Formula: How rogues, geniuses, and speed freaks reengineered F1 into the world's fastestgrowing sport. Monoray.

Rogers, E. M. (2003). Diffusion of innovations (5th ed.). Free Press.

Schumpeter, J. A. (1942). Capitalism, socialism, and democracy. Harper & Brothers.

Schein, E. H. (2010). Organizational culture and leadership (4th ed.). JosseyBass.

Sen, A. (1999). Development as freedom. Oxford University Press.

Shepherd, A. (2025). 15 company culture books that define modern leadership. Retrieved from https://bookauthority.org

Senge, P. M. (1990). The fifth discipline: The art & practice of the learning organization. Doubleday.

Smith, A. D. (1991). National identity. University of Nevada Press.

Tomlinson, J. (1999). Globalization and culture. University of Chicago Press.

Triandis, H. C. (1995). Individualism and collectivism. Westview Press.

Waterman, R. H., Peters, T. J., & Phillips, J. R. (1980). Structure is not organization. Business Horizons, 23(3), 14–26.

Wiese, S. A., Lehmann, J., & Beckmann, M. (2024). Organizational culture and the usage of Industry 4.0 technologies: Evidence from Swiss businesses. arXiv. https://arxiv.org/abs/2412.12752

Chapter 3: It's Not the One Right Culture, but the Strong Culture

Achievers. (n.d.). Organizational culture: Definition, importance, and development. Retrieved from https://www.achievers.com/blog/organizational-culture-definition/

BMW Group. (2025). Our culture & values. BMW Group Careers. Retrieved February 8, 2025, from https://www.bmwgroup.jobs/us/en/culture.html

Cole, B. M., & Salimath, M. S. (2013). Diversity identity management: An organizational perspective. Journal of Business Ethics, 116(1), 151–161.

Deal, T. E., & Kennedy, A. A. (2000). Corporate cultures: The rites and rituals of corporate life (2nd ed.). Perseus Publishing.

Deshpandé, R., Farley, J. U., & Webster, F. E. (1993). Corporate culture, customer orientation, and innovativeness in Japanese firms: A quadrad analysis. Journal of Marketing, 57(1), 23–37.

Garvin, D. A. (2013). How Google sold its engineers on management. Harvard Business Review. Retrieved from https://hbr.org/2013/12/how-google-sold-its-engineers-on-management

Google. (2025). Our culture. Google Careers. Retrieved February 8, 2025, from https://careers.google.com/culture/

Humanizing Work. (n.d.). Decision making in consensus-driven cultures. Retrieved from https://www.humanizingwork.com/decision-making-in-consensus-driven-cultures/

Jassawalla, A. R., & Sashittal, H. C. (2002). Cultures that support product-innovation processes. Academy of Management Executive, 16(3), 42–54.

Lencioni, P. (2002). The five dysfunctions of a team: A leadership fable. Jossey-Bass.

Pallister, B. C. (n.d.). Embedding value into organizations using the innovation value pyramid. Retrieved from https://www.academia.edu/Embedding_Value_into_Organisations_Using_the_Innovation_Value_Pyramid

Panmore Institute. (2017). Google's (Alphabet's) organizational culture & its traits. Panmore Institute Business Management. Retrieved from https://panmore.com/googles-organizational-culture-characteristics

Prather, C. W., & Turrell, M. C. (2002). Involve everyone in the innovation process. Research-Technology Management, 45(5), 13–16.

Robertson, B. J. (2015). Holacracy: The new management system for a rapidly changing world. Henry Holt and Company.

SAS Institute. (n.d.). Workplace culture. Retrieved from https://www.sas.com/en_us/company-information/workplace-culture.html

Schein, E. H. (2010). Organizational culture and leadership (4th ed.). Jossey-Bass.

Spyre Group. (n.d.). The impact of organizational culture on innovation. Retrieved from https://www.spyre.group/post/unlocking-growth-the-impact-of-organizational-culture-on-innovation

Stewart, T. A. (2006). The wealth of knowledge: Intellectual capital and the twenty-first century organization. Crown Business.

Stone, B. (2013). The everything store: Jeff Bezos and the age of Amazon. Little, Brown and Company.

Vance, A. (2015). Elon Musk: Tesla, SpaceX, and the quest for a fantastic future. Ecco.

WalkMe Team. (2024, July 23). How does organizational culture impact the change process? Retrieved from https://www.walkme.com/blog/how-does-organizational-culture-impact-the-change-process/

W. L. Gore & Associates. (n.d.). Culture. Retrieved from https://www.gore.com/about/culture

Wingfield, N. (2023, July 17). Amazon Prime Day contributed to a surge in warehouse injuries, Senate probe finds. The Wall Street Journal. Retrieved February 8, 2025, from https://www.wsj.com/business/amazon-prime-day-senate-probe-warehouse-injuries-da3c6dbe

Chapter 4: Intentionally Creating Culture: Building a Roadmap and Master Plan

Edmondson, A. C. (2018). The Fearless Organization: Creating Psychological Safety in the Workplace for Learning, Innovation, and Growth. Wiley.
Frei, F., & Morriss, A. (2020). Unleashed: The Unapologetic Leader's Guide to Empowering Everyone Around You. Harvard Business Review Press.
Groysberg, B., Lee, J., Price, J., & Cheng, J. (2018). The Leader's Guide to Corporate Culture. Harvard Business Review, 96(1), 44–52.
Heath, C., & Heath, D. (2010). Switch: How to Change Things When Change Is Hard. Broadway Books.
Johnson, G., Whittington, R., Scholes, K., Angwin, D., & Regnér, P. (2017). Exploring Strategy: Text and Cases. Pearson.
Kegan, R., & Lahey, L. L. (2016). An Everyone Culture: Becoming a Deliberately Developmental Organization. Harvard Business Review Press.
Laloux, F. (2014). Reinventing Organizations: A Guide to Creating Organizations Inspired by the Next Stage of Human Consciousness. Nelson Parker.
Lorsch, J. W., & McTague, E. (2016). Culture is Not the Culprit. Harvard Business Review, 94(4), 96–105.

Nadella, S., Shaw, G., & Nichols, J. T. (2017). Hit Refresh: The Quest to Rediscover Microsoft's Soul and Imagine a Better Future for Everyone. Harper Business.

Schein, E. H., & Schein, P. (2017). Organizational Culture and Leadership (5th ed.). Wiley.

Sinek, S. (2019). The Infinite Game. Portfolio.

Watkins, M. D. (2013). The First 90 Days: Proven Strategies for Getting Up to Speed Faster and Smarter. Harvard Business Review Press.

Chapter 5: Igniting Organizational Heartbeat Engagement: Discretionary Effort, Loyalty, and Advocacy

Buckingham, M., & Coffman, C. (1999). First, break all the rules: What the world's greatest managers do differently. Simon & Schuster.

Catmull, E., & Wallace, A. (2014). Creativity, Inc.: Overcoming the unseen forces that stand in the way of true inspiration. Ballantine Books.

Deal, T. E., & Kennedy, A. A. (1982). Corporate cultures: The rites and rituals of corporate life. Addison-Wesley.

Janis, I. L. (1972). Victims of groupthink. Houghton Mifflin.

Khurana, R. (2007). From higher aims to hired hands: The social transformation of American business schools. Harvard Business Press.

Page, S. E. (2007). The difference: How the power of diversity creates better groups, firms, schools, and societies. Princeton University Press.

Schein, E. H. (2010). Organizational culture and leadership (4th ed.). Jossey-Bass.

Chapter 6: Case Studies: Lessons from Strong Cultures

2819 Church. (n.d.). About our mission. Retrieved March 22, 2025, from 2819church.org

Al Rajhi Bank. (2024). Fourth quarter 2024 earnings release. https://www.alrajhibank.com.sa

Alphabet Inc. (2024). Q4 2023 earnings report. Retrieved from https://abc.xyz/investor

Amazon.com, Inc. (2024). Annual report 2023. Retrieved from https://www.aboutamazon.com/investor-relations

Bayley, D. H. (1991). Forces of order: Policing modern Japan. University of California Press.

Bharat Biotech. (n.d.). Company overview and mission. https://www.bharatbiotech.com

Branson, R. (2006). Screw it, let's do it: Lessons in life and business. Virgin Books.

Branson, R. (2011). Screw business as usual. Portfolio.

Branson, R. (2014). The Virgin way: Everything I know about leadership. Portfolio.

Branson, R. (2017). Finding my virginity: The new autobiography. Portfolio/Penguin.

Business Insider. (2022). Chick-fil-A's Sunday closure and revenue impact. https://www.businessinsider.com

Cameron, K. S., & Quinn, R. E. (2011). Diagnosing and changing organizational culture (3rd ed.). Wiley.

Chick-fil-A. (n.d.). Company purpose and corporate values. https://www.chick-fil-a.com

Chung, H., & Luo, Y. (2013). Samsung's competitive strategy and organizational culture. Journal of Business Research, 66(1), 65–72.

Confucius. (1998). The analects (R. Dawson, Trans.). Oxford University Press. (Original work published c. 500 BCE)

Davis, R. C., Henderson, N. J., & Merrick, C. (2003). Community policing: Variations on the Western model in Japan and the United States. Police Practice and Research, 4(2), 103–121. https://doi.org/10.1080/1561426032000115827

Fackler, M. (2007, November 6). Policing in Japan: Not just a job, but a way of life. The New York Times. https://www.nytimes.com

Forbes. (2024). Al Rajhi Bank company profile. https://www.forbes.com/companies/al-rajhi-bank

Forever 21. (n.d.). Company history and founders' faith influence. https://www.forever21.com

Fortune. (2023). Fortune Global 500 list. Retrieved from https://fortune.com/global500/

Glassdoor. (2023). Best Places to Work 2023. Retrieved from https://www.glassdoor.com/Award/Best-Places-to-Work-LST_KQ0,19.htm

Global Firepower. (2024). Military strength ranking 2024. Retrieved from https://www.globalfirepower.com

Goffee, R., & Jones, G. (2015). Why should anyone work here? What it takes to create an authentic organization. Harvard Business Review Press.

Grant, A. (2013). Give and take: Why helping others drives our success. Viking.

Hamel, G., & Zanini, M. (2020). Humanocracy: Creating organizations as amazing as the people inside them. Harvard Business Review Press.

Harvard University. (2024). World university rankings 2024. Retrieved from https://www.harvard.edu

Hobby Lobby. (n.d.). Our company. https://www.hobbylobby.com

Hofstede Insights. (2024). Country comparison: China, United States. https://www.hofstede-insights.com/country-comparison/china,the-usa/

IKEA. (2023). IKEA sustainability report and financial overview. Retrieved from https://www.ingka.com

In-N-Out Burger. (n.d.). About us and cultural values. https://www.in-n-out.com

JCB Group. (n.d.). Company history and founder values. https://www.jcb.com

Kotter, J. P. (2012). Leading change. Harvard Business Review Press.

Lakewood Church. (n.d.). Our ministry. Retrieved March 22, 2025, from https://www.lakewoodchurch.com

Lencioni, P. (2002). The five dysfunctions of a team: A leadership fable. Jossey-Bass.

Murugappa Group. (n.d.). Our values and history. https://www.murugappa.com

New York Police Department. (2023). Annual firearms discharge report. Retrieved from https://www.nyc.gov/assets/nypd/downloads/pdf/use-of-force/annual-firearms-discharge-report-2023.pdf

Osteen, J. (2004). Your best life now: 7 steps to living at your full potential. FaithWords.

Peking University. (2024). Academic profile. Retrieved from https://english.pku.edu.cn

Reichel, P. L. (2018). Comparative criminal justice systems: A topical approach (7th ed.). Pearson.

Schein, E. H. (2010). Organizational culture and leadership (4th ed.). Jossey-Bass.

Schein, E. H., & Schein, P. (2016). Organizational culture and leadership (5th ed.). Wiley.

ServiceMaster. (n.d.). Our heritage and principles. https://www.servicemaster.com

Siemens AG. (2023). Annual report 2023. Retrieved from https://www.siemens.com/global/en/company/investor-relations/financial-publications/annual-reports.html

Siemens AG. (2023). Sustainability and people strategy. Retrieved from https://www.siemens.com

Siemens AG. (n.d.). What we do. Retrieved March 22, 2025, from https://www.siemens.com/global/en/company/about/what-we-do.html

Statista. (2024). Chick-fil-A U.S. sales data and average unit volume. https://www.statista.com

Stone, B. (2013). The everything store: Jeff Bezos and the age of Amazon. Little, Brown and Company.

Supreme Court of the United States. (2014). Burwell v. Hobby Lobby Stores, Inc., 573 U.S. 682.

Tokyo Metropolitan Police Department. (2023). Organization and duties. Retrieved from https://www.keishicho.metro.tokyo.lg.jp

Toyota Motor Corporation. (n.d.). Toyota Production System (TPS) and Kaizen principles. https://www.toyota-global.com

Trinity Mirror Archives. (n.d.). Historical ethical foundations and business practices.

Tsinghua University. (2024). Global university rankings 2024. Retrieved from https://www.tsinghua.edu.cn

United Nations. (n.d.). Member states. Retrieved March 22, 2025, from https://www.un.org/en/about-us/member-states

Unilever. (n.d.). Company purpose and sustainability strategy. https://www.unilever.com

U.S. Department of Justice. (2022). NYPD and use of force: Reports and recommendations. Retrieved from https://www.justice.gov

Virgin Group. (2023). About us. Retrieved from https://www.virgin.com/about-virgin/virgin-group

Virgin Group. (2023). Our brands. Retrieved from https://www.virgin.com/about-virgin/our-brands

Virgin Group. (n.d.). Our brand and culture. https://www.virgin.com

World Bank. (2024). GDP (current US$) - United States, China. Retrieved from https://data.worldbank.org

World Intellectual Property Organization. (2023). Global Innovation Index 2023. Retrieved from https://www.wipo.int/global_innovation_index

Chapter 7: Transforming Culture: Recognizing When Change is Needed

Bridges, W. (2009). Managing transitions: Making the most of change (3rd ed.). Da Capo Press.

Cameron, K. S., & Quinn, R. E. (2011). Diagnosing and changing organizational culture: Based on the competing values framework (3rd ed.). Jossey-Bass.

Hiatt, J. M. (2006). ADKAR: A model for change in business, government and our community. Prosci Learning Center Publications.

Kaplan, R. S., & Norton, D. P. (2008). The execution premium: Linking strategy to operations for competitive advantage. Harvard Business Press.

Kotter, J. P. (2012). Leading change. Harvard Business Review Press.

Lawler, E. E., & Worley, C. G. (2006). Built to change: How to achieve sustained organizational effectiveness. Jossey-Bass.

McKinsey & Company. (2008). The 7S framework. Retrieved from https://www.mckinsey.com/business-functions/organization/our-insights/enduring-ideas-the-7-s-framework

Morgan, J. (2017). The employee experience advantage: How to win the war for talent by giving employees the workspaces they want, the tools they need, and a culture they can celebrate. Wiley.

Pfeffer, J., & Sutton, R. I. (2006). Hard facts, dangerous half-truths, and total nonsense: Profiting from evidence-based management. Harvard Business Review Press.

Schein, E. H., & Schein, P. A. (2016). Organizational culture and leadership (5th ed.). Wiley.

Ulrich, D., Brockbank, W., Johnson, D., Sandholtz, K., & Younger, J. (2008). HR competencies: Mastery at the intersection of people and business. Society for Human Resource Management.

Waterman, R. H., Peters, T. J., & Phillips, J. R. (1980). Structure is not organization. Business Horizons, 23(3), 14–26.

Wellins, R. S., Bernthal, P., & Phelps, M. (2005). Employee engagement: The key to realizing competitive advantage. Development Dimensions International.

Chapter 8: The Impact of the Coronavirus Pandemic on Culture

BetterUp Labs. (2021). The connection crisis: Why community matters in the new world of work. BetterUp. https://www.betterup.com

Edelman. (2023). Edelman Trust Barometer 2023. Edelman. https://www.edelman.com/trust-barometer

Gallup. (2023). State of the Global Workplace: 2023 Report. Gallup. https://www.gallup.com/workplace/349484/state-of-the-global-workplace.aspx

Harvard Business Review. (2021). The most admired leadership traits in hybrid environments. Harvard Business Publishing. https://hbr.org

Pew Research Center. (2022, September 20). More Americans are moving abroad. Why? Pew Research Center. https://www.pewresearch.org

World Health Organization. (2021). COVID-19 pandemic triggers 25% increase in prevalence of anxiety and depression worldwide. https://www.who.int/news/item/02-03-2022

United Nations Development Programme. (2020). Human development perspectives: COVID-19 and human development. https://hdr.undp.org/content/covid-19-and-human-development

U.S. Bureau of Labor Statistics. (2022). Job openings and labor turnover survey highlights. https://www.bls.gov

World Bank. (2022). COVID-19 to add as many as 150 million extreme poor by 2021. https://www.worldbank.org

Chapter 9: Generative AI and Its Impact on Culture: The New Presence in the Room

Binns, R. (2018). Fairness in machine learning: Lessons from political philosophy. Communications of the ACM, 61(5), 82–89. https://doi.org/10.1145/3236346

Brynjolfsson, E., & McAfee, A. (2014). The second machine age: Work, progress, and prosperity in a time of brilliant technologies. W. W. Norton & Company.

Brynjolfsson, E., & McAfee, A. (2017). Machine, platform, crowd: Harnessing our digital future. W. W. Norton & Company.

Davenport, T. H., & Ronanki, R. (2018). Artificial intelligence for the real world. Harvard Business Review, 96(1), 108–116.

Dignum, V. (2019). Responsible artificial intelligence: How to develop and use AI in a responsible way. Springer. https://doi.org/10.1007/978-3-030-30371-6

Eubanks, V. (2018). Automating inequality: How high-tech tools profile, police, and punish the poor. St. Martin's Press.

Frey, C. B., & Osborne, M. A. (2017). The future of employment: How susceptible are jobs to computerization? Technological Forecasting and Social Change, 114, 254–280. https://doi.org/10.1016/j.techfore.2016.08.019

International Energy Agency. (2023). Data centres and data transmission networks. https://www.iea.org/reports/data-centres-and-data-transmission-networks

International Monetary Fund. (2020). World Economic Outlook: A Long and Difficult Ascent. https://www.imf.org/en/Publications/WEO

Manyika, J., Chui, M., Miremadi, M., Bughin, J., George, K., Willmott, P., & Dewhurst, M. (2017). A future that works: Automation, employment, and productivity. McKinsey Global Institute. https://www.mckinsey.com/featured-insights/digital-disruption/harnessing-automation-for-a-future-that-works

Microsoft. (2023). 2023 Environmental Sustainability Report. https://www.microsoft.com/en-us/sustainability

Mokyr, J., Vickers, C., & Ziebarth, N. L. (2015). The history of technological anxiety and the future of economic growth: Is this time different? Journal of Economic Perspectives, 29(3), 31–50. https://doi.org/10.1257/jep.29.3.31

Nature. (2023). Large language models can hallucinate facts. Nature Machine Intelligence, 5(10), 1002–1004. https://doi.org/10.1038/s42256-023-00784-9

O'Neil, C. (2016). Weapons of math destruction: How big data increases inequality and threatens democracy. Crown Publishing Group.

Pew Research Center. (2020). The American middle class: Stable in size, but losing ground financially. https://www.pewresearch.org/social-trends/2020/01/09/the-american-middle-class/

Raisch, S., Krakowski, S., Seidel, V. P., & Berente, N. (2023). Artificial intelligence and the cultural transformation of organizations. Academy of Management Review, 48(1), 37–62. https://doi.org/10.5465/amr.2020.0285

Rifkin, J. (2014). The zero marginal cost society: The internet of things, the collaborative commons, and the eclipse of capitalism. Palgrave Macmillan.

Schwab, K. (2017). The fourth industrial revolution. Crown Business.

Smith, M., & Anderson, J. (2014). AI, robotics, and the future of jobs. Pew Research Center. https://www.pewresearch.org/internet/2014/08/06/future-of-jobs/

Stanford University. (2024). AI Index Report 2024. Stanford Institute for Human-Centered Artificial Intelligence. https://aiindex.stanford.edu

Vaccari, C., & Chadwick, A. (2020). Deepfakes and disinformation: Exploring the impact of synthetic political video on deception, uncertainty, and trust in news. Social Media + Society, 6(1), 1–13. https://doi.org/10.1177/2056305120903408

West, D. M. (2018). The future of work: Robots, AI, and automation. Brookings Institution Press.

Winfield, A. F., & Jirotka, M. (2018). Ethical governance is essential to building trust in robotics and artificial intelligence systems. Philosophical Transactions of the Royal Society A: Mathematical, Physical and Engineering Sciences, 376(2133), 20180085. https://doi.org/10.1098/rsta.2018.0085

World Economic Forum. (2024). Global Risks Report 2024. https://www.weforum.org/reports/global-risks-report-2024

Yang, A. (2018). The war on normal people: The truth about America's disappearing jobs and why Universal Basic Income is our future. Hachette Books.

Chapter 10 The Death of Diversity in the US?

Boston Consulting Group. (2020). How diverse leadership teams boost innovation. https://www.bcg.com/publications/2020/diverse-leadership-teams-boost-innovation

Gilligan, C. (1982). In a different voice: Psychological theory and women's development. Harvard University Press.

Greene, A. (2024). Personal ethical values in diversity management: The role of moral motivation. Journal of Business Ethics. https://doi.org/10.1007/s10551-023-05514-w

Hayvon, J. C. (2024). Action against inequalities: A synthesis of social justice and EDI theories, models, and frameworks. International Journal for Equity in Health, 23(1). https://doi.org/10.1186/s12939-024-02141-3

Investopedia. (2023). How the veil of ignorance impacts the principle of fairness. https://www.investopedia.com/veil-of-ignorance-and-the-principle-of-fairness-7508086

Kaszner, C. (2022). Social justice and the radical diversity approach. Genealogy Critique, 8(1), 12–29. https://www.genealogy-critique.net/article/id/9235/

Lafferty, D. J. R. (2024). A path forward: Creating an academic culture of justice. Bulletin of the Ecological Society of America, 105(3), e02117. https://doi.org/10.1002/bes2.2117

McKinsey & Company. (2020). Diversity wins: How inclusion matters. https://www.mckinsey.com/featured-insights/diversity-and-inclusion/diversity-wins-how-inclusion-matters

Pew Research Center. (2020). The American middle class: Stable in size, but losing ground financially. https://www.pewresearch.org/social-trends/2020/01/09/the-american-middle-class/

Pew Research Center. (2023). Most Americans say having a diverse community strengthens the country. https://www.pewresearch.org

Rawls, J. (1971). A theory of justice. Belknap Press.

Walzer, M. (1983). Spheres of justice: A defense of pluralism and equality. Basic Books.

Young, I. M. (1990). Justice and the politics of difference. Princeton University Press.

Chapter 11: Future State of Work and Impact on Culture

Brynjolfsson, E., & McAfee, A. (2014). The second machine age: Work, progress, and prosperity in a time of brilliant technologies. W.W. Norton & Company.

Deloitte. (2023). 2023 Global Human Capital Trends: New fundamentals for a boundaryless world. Deloitte Insights. https://www2.deloitte.com/insights/us/en/focus/human-capital-trends.html

Frey, C. B., & Osborne, M. A. (2017). The future of employment: How susceptible are jobs to computerization? Technological Forecasting and Social Change, 114, 254–280. https://doi.org/10.1016/j.techfore.2016.08.019

IBM. (2024). What is quantum computing? IBM Quantum. https://www.ibm.com/quantum-computing/learn/what-is-quantum-computing/

International Labor Organization. (2021). Working from home: From invisibility to decent work. https://www.ilo.org/global/publications/books/WCMS_765806/lang--en/index.htm

McKinsey & Company. (2023). The State of Organizations 2023: Ten shifts transforming organizations. https://www.mckinsey.com/capabilities/people-and-organizational-performance/our-insights/the-state-of-organizations-2023

Microsoft WorkLab. (2023). Work Trend Index: Will AI fix work? https://www.microsoft.com/en-us/worklab/work-trend-index/ai-at-work-2023

OECD. (2021). The future of work: OECD employment outlook 2021. https://www.oecd.org/employment-outlook/

Pew Research Center. (2022). The gig worker next door: Understanding gig work in the U.S. https://www.pewresearch.org/social-trends/2022/12/08/the-gig-worker-next-door/

Susskind, D. (2020). A world without work: Technology, automation, and how we should respond. Metropolitan Books.

World Economic Forum. (2023). The Future of Jobs Report 2023. https://www.weforum.org/reports/the-future-of-jobs-report-2023/

Chapter 12. Defining & Operationalizing Culture Strength

Cameron, K. S., & Quinn, R. E. (2011). Diagnosing and changing organizational culture: Based on the competing values framework (3rd ed.). Jossey-Bass.

Denison, D. R. (1990). Corporate culture and organizational effectiveness. Wiley.

Denison, D. R., Nieminen, L. R., & Kotrba, L. M. (2014). Diagnosing organizational cultures: A conceptual and empirical review of culture effectiveness surveys. European Journal of Work and Organizational Psychology, 23(1), 145–161. https://doi.org/10.1080/1359432X.2012.713173

Groysberg, B., Lee, J., Price, J., & Cheng, J. Y. J. (2018). The leader's guide to corporate culture. Harvard Business Review, 96(1), 44–52.

Kotter, J. P., & Heskett, J. L. (1992). Corporate culture and performance. Free Press.

Reina, C. S., Rogers, K. M., Peterson, S. J., Byron, K., & Hom, P. W. (2018). Quitting the boss? The role of manager influence tactics and employee emotional engagement in voluntary turnover. Journal of Leadership & Organizational Studies, 25(1), 5–18. https://doi.org/10.1177/1548051817709007

Schein, E. H., & Schein, P. A. (2017). Organizational culture and leadership (5th ed.). Wiley.

Schneider, B., Ehrhart, M. G., & Macey, W. H. (2013). Organizational climate and culture. Annual Review of Psychology, 64, 361–388. https://doi.org/10.1146/annurev-psych-113011-143809

Van Veenendaal, A., & Bondarouk, T. (2022). Measuring organizational culture: Review of instruments and approaches. Journal of Organizational Effectiveness: People and Performance, 9(1), 84–104. https://doi.org/10.1108/JOEPP-04-2021-0036

Chapter 13. Conclusion: You Choose–Intentionally Maintaining a Strong Culture or Playing Organizational Russian Roulette

Block, P. (2013). Stewardship: Choosing service over self-interest (2nd ed.). Berrett-Koehler.

Cameron, K. S. (2008). Positive leadership: Strategies for extraordinary performance. Berrett-Koehler.

Collins, J. (2001). Good to great: Why some companies make the leap and others don't. HarperCollins.

Kotter, J. P. (1996). Leading change. Harvard Business School Press.

Lencioni, P. (2002). The five dysfunctions of a team: A leadership fable. Jossey-Bass.

Schein, E. H., & Schein, P. A. (2017). Organizational culture and leadership (5th ed.). Wiley.

Watkins, M. D. (2013). What is organizational culture? And why should we care? Harvard Business Review Digital Articles, 1–5.

Weick, K. E., & Sutcliffe, K. M. (2015). Managing the unexpected: Resilient performance in an age of uncertainty (3rd ed.). Wiley.

Appendix Two:
References

Cole, A. (2013). Understanding organizational identity and culture. Management Decision, 51(3), 643–660. https://doi.org/10.1108/00251741311309613

Deal, T. E., & Kennedy, A. A. (2000). Corporate cultures: The rites and rituals of corporate life. Perseus Books.

Deshpandé, R., Farley, J. U., & Webster, F. E. (1993). Corporate culture, customer orientation, and innovativeness in Japanese firms: A quadrad analysis. Journal of Marketing, 57(1), 23–37. https://doi.org/10.1177/002224299305700102

Garvin, D. A. (2013). How Google sold its engineers on management. Harvard Business Review, 91(12), 74–82.

Prather, C. W., & Turrell, M. C. (2002). Involve everyone: Improving products, services, and processes through organization-wide suggestion systems. Productivity Press.

Robertson, B. (2015). Holacracy: The new management system for a rapidly changing world. Henry Holt and Company.

Schein, E. H. (2010). Organizational culture and leadership (4th ed.). Jossey-Bass.

Stone, D., Patton, B., & Heen, S. (2010). Difficult conversations: How to discuss what matters most. Penguin.

WalkMe Team. (2024). Digital adoption strategies: Aligning brand presence with organizational culture. WalkMe Inc. https://www.walkme.com/resources/

INDEX

- ROI of culture 251
- accountability 252
- advocacy 249
- alignment 252-253, 255
- alignment with values 253
- approach 251
- autonomy 250
- balanced-intensity culture 248
- behavioral consistency 247
- behavioral reinforcement 253
- business alignment 252
- clarity 248-250, 252, 255
- collaboration 254
- communication 254
- community impact 254
- consistency 24, 26-27, 30, 33, 37, 43, 46-48, 52, 60, 62, 69, 71, 73-75, 84-85, 87, 90, 98-101, 103, 105, 107, 109-110, 113-114, 117, 120, 122, 125, 173, 191-192, 196, 214, 216
- constructive 94, 96
- crisis response 253
- cultural alignment 250
- cultural change 254
- cultural clarity 253

- cultural imprint 250
- cultural seal 247
- culture of growth 251
- customer obsession 247
- customer service 255
- decision rights 252
- decision-making 248
- definition 248
- deliberate culture 251
- design culture 247
- desired results 252
- development 251
- diagnostics 254
- discipline 249
- discretionary effort 249
- distance 252
- emotional connection 251
- employee growth 249
- engagement 253-254
- ethics 251
- execution 18, 32, 37, 55-56, 72, 76-77, 135, 189, 231
- experience 249
- fairness 249

- feedback loops 248
- foundation 254
- frameworks 254
- healthy culture 250
- hierarchy 254
- high-intensity culture 247
- impact 248
- inclusion 249
- innovation 247, 250
- innovation culture 250
- integration with culture 253
- intensity 24, 26, 35, 48-50, 244
- internal vs external alignment 247
- leadership 247, 249-251, 254
- leadership coaching 249
- leadership courage 250
- leadership credibility 247
- leadership decisions 251
- levels of culture 253
- long-term culture 254
- loyalty 249
- management 254

- mapping 253
- measurement 251
- navigation 248
- operationalization .... I, 245, 251
- operationalized 17, 31, 245
- organizational 250
- orientation 249
- outcomes 250
- performance 251
- pipelines 254
- precision 247
- programs 252
- purpose clarity 58, 245
- quality 247
- readiness 58, 80-81, 128, 245
- real-time 45, 66, 70, 194, 245
- recognition 252
- reinforced 26, 41, 57, 69, 86, 103, 130, 145, 168, 196, 201, 245
- reinforcement 248, 252
- relationships 250, 254
- representation 249
- risk tolerance 34, 58, 246

- rituals 19, 20, 36, 39, 42, 62-64, 69-70, 77, 82, 86, 99, 114, 135, 140, 145-146, 150-151, 155-156, 164, 190, 193-196, 199-201, 209, 212, 223, 226, 240, 246, 252

- scaling 250

- service values 248

- shared 248, 250, 253

- shared identity 248

- shared practices 253

- social fabric 253

- spectrum 253

- strategic clarity 247

- strategy alignment 249

- style 249

- styles 248

- sustainability 252

- systems 249, 252

- talent 251

- traditions 253

- transparency 248

- trust 247-248, 250-251, 253-254

- trust building 247

- trust-building 248

- values 247, 252

- values alignment 252

- values in practice 247

Accountability 11, 33, 38, 40, 42, 48-50, 57, 64, 71, 83, 91, 94, 99, 105, 113, 117-119, 121-122, 133, 140, 144-145, 147, 176, 179, 194, 200, 202, 213-215, 220, 224, 252

Alignment 25, 31, 33-34, 36-37, 43, 46, 48-49, 51-52, 54, 58-60, 63, 69-70, 72-73, 75-76, 78, 81, 86-89, 91, 93, 95, 97, 100, 114-115, 124-126, 128, 133, 136, 139, 144, 146-147, 150, 156-157, 163, 172, 178, 182, 186, 188, 191, 194-196, 198, 201, 204-206, 208-209, 212, 214-216, 218, 220-222, 224, 247, 249-250, 252-253, 255

Amazon 30, 54, 109-112, 129, 158, 228-229, 231, 234, 247

Apple 10, 247

Authenticity 35, 75, 77, 95, 97, 116, 129, 140, 150, 159, 247

Authority 26, 62, 113, 116, 120-121, 134, 153, 159, 176, 247

Bias 34, 164, 168, 171, 176, 247

Bmw 227, 247

Branding 31, 50-52, 56, 75, 108, 127, 150, 175, 182, 247

Career 62, 108, 215, 247

Change 9-10, 13, 19, 23, 27, 30-32, 35, 37, 39, 48, 62, 77, 79-80, 84, 87, 129-130, 134-139, 141-143, 146, 150, 152, 158, 165-166, 176-177, 179, 196, 201-204, 221-222, 224-225, 229, 233, 235, 237, 241, 243, 245, 254

Chick-fil-a 10, 54, 126, 128-129, 193, 231, 234, 248

Collaboration 26, 29, 33-34, 38, 41, 45-47, 49, 62, 91, 103, 116, 124, 132, 137-140, 145, 173, 197, 221, 248, 254

Communication 38, 51, 58-59, 62, 68, 71-72, 79-80, 82, 85-86, 89, 106, 121, 123-125, 142, 147, 198, 203, 212, 214, 220, 222, 248, 254

Community 17, 24, 39, 45, 50-51, 58, 63, 75-76, 113, 115, 117-122, 146-148, 153-155, 157, 177, 179-180, 235-236, 240, 245, 248, 254

Conflict 25, 35, 40, 43-44, 47, 49, 53-54, 100, 121, 123, 125, 132, 147, 214, 221, 248

Consistency 12, 28, 30-31, 34, 37, 41, 47, 50-52, 56, 64, 66, 75, 77-78, 88-89, 91, 94, 102-105, 107, 109, 111, 113-114, 117-118, 121, 124, 126, 129, 177, 195-196, 200, 218, 220, 224, 247-248

Culture 7, 9-13, 15-43, 45-61, 64-71, 73-78, 81, 83-84, 88-118, 120-121, 123-150, 153, 155-157, 159-160, 162-168, 171-173, 175-178, 180-210, 212, 214-218, 220-222, 224-231, 233-236, 240, 242-245, 247-248, 250-251, 253-255

Customer 10, 30, 38, 43, 50, 52, 54, 63, 76, 87-88, 106, 108-109, 112, 116, 122, 135, 161, 175, 178, 194, 203, 227, 244, 247, 249, 255

Decision-making 16, 28, 31, 33, 38, 62, 64-65, 70-71, 86, 90-91, 114, 116, 125, 147, 159, 191, 195, 214, 218, 220, 224, 227, 248-249

Development 38, 42-45, 62, 69, 71-72, 74, 77, 81-82, 84, 111, 114, 116, 140, 199, 214-215, 226-227, 236, 239, 245, 249, 251

Diversity 7, 9, 34, 52, 97, 100, 131-133, 169-183, 186, 191, 227, 230, 239-240, 249

Engagement..7, 12, 19-22, 25, 36, 46-47, 50, 58-59, 69, 75-76, 79-83, 85, 87, 92-97, 101, 136, 142, 147, 152, 192-193, 195-196, 201-203, 205-206, 209-210, 212, 217, 221, 224, 230, 236, 242, 245, 249, 253-254

Equity 40, 45, 50, 63, 167, 169-171, 179, 183, 194, 197, 201, 239, 249

Execution..22, 36, 59-60, 76, 80-81, 139, 193, 235, 249, 253

Feedback..26, 35, 40, 43-44, 47, 49, 52-54, 57-58, 60, 64, 71-72, 74-75, 82-83, 85-87, 94, 98, 133, 140-148, 164, 167, 195, 197-198, 213-214, 217, 220-222, 224, 248

Goals...10, 17, 19, 57, 59, 69, 87, 92, 99, 102, 104, 125, 133, 136, 140, 184, 189, 250

Google...10, 17, 30, 109-112, 129, 188, 193, 227-228, 244, 250

Growth 28, 38, 42-45, 52, 62, 76-77, 90, 99, 119, 125, 135, 140, 147, 174-175, 178-179, 188, 202-203, 206, 222, 225, 228-229, 238, 245, 249-251

Health 16, 40, 51, 57, 79, 108, 154-158, 185, 188, 217, 222, 236, 239, 250

Honesty 10, 12, 71, 79, 183, 214, 218-219, 250

Identity 12, 24, 36, 42, 51, 53, 66, 75-76, 88, 90, 94, 103-104, 106, 115, 118-119, 123, 127, 150, 153, 155, 157-159, 165, 167, 170-171, 174-175, 177-178, 180, 188, 190, 196, 199, 202, 204, 208-209, 213, 216, 226-227, 244, 248, 250

Inclusion 25, 39-40, 44-45, 48-49, 53, 69, 103, 131-133, 136, 139, 146-147, 149, 170-171, 176, 182-183, 186, 190-191, 240, 249-250

Innovation 25, 30-31, 33, 37-38, 46-47, 54, 63, 69, 84, 87-88, 90, 95, 100, 105-106, 108-113, 115-116, 123-125, 132-133, 135, 137-140, 146-147, 161, 173, 178, 183, 193-194, 199, 201, 203, 217, 221, 227-229, 234, 239, 245, 247, 250

Integrity 39, 42, 46, 48-49, 71, 77, 94-95, 105, 111, 115, 121-122, 128-129, 148, 176, 179-180, 187, 196, 199

Intentionality 34-35, 64, 90-91, 106, 193, 210, 251

Leadership...23, 25-26, 28-32, 34, 36-38, 41-42, 48, 56-58, 60-61, 63, 68-69, 71-72, 75, 81-83, 85-86, 88-90, 106-109, 113, 116, 123-125, 132-137, 139-140, 142, 145-146, 148-150, 160-161, 164, 166, 170, 173, 175-177, 179-182, 187, 191, 197-200, 202, 204-206, 210, 212, 214, 218, 220, 222-224, 226, 228, 230-231, 233, 235-236, 239, 242-245, 247, 249-251, 254

Learning 26, 33, 38, 40, 43, 46, 62, 71-74, 77, 142-143, 162, 166, 217, 222-223, 226, 229, 235, 237, 251

Loyalty...7, 12, 52, 54, 91-94, 97-98, 101, 103, 112-113, 116, 124-126, 155, 159, 178, 185, 187-188, 191-192, 195, 230, 249, 251

Management...62, 77, 79-80, 84, 90, 110, 173, 196, 206, 212, 214, 216, 221-222, 224, 227-228, 235, 238-239, 244, 251, 254

Mentoring 43, 53, 62, 133, 251

Metrics 24, 28, 44, 47, 60, 64-65, 70, 73-74, 76, 78-79, 84, 86-90, 131-133, 136, 142, 147, 159, 173, 182, 194, 200-205, 208, 215, 219-222, 224, 251

Mission..17, 24, 29, 39, 44, 53, 59, 69, 81, 90, 98-100, 107, 111, 113-116, 126, 129, 139, 146-147, 179-180, 192, 194, 213, 231, 251

Motivation 47, 92, 117, 219, 239

Nps 17, 161, 252

Operationalization 9, 13, 252

Outcomes 10, 13, 15, 17, 19, 22, 48, 58, 69, 93, 121, 138, 140, 147-148, 181, 189, 191, 200-205, 218, 221, 224, 250, 252

Patagonia 50, 252

Performance 22, 24, 26, 31, 35-36, 43, 45-48, 50, 52, 56, 61-62, 65, 69, 73-74, 87-88, 90, 96, 99, 105, 109, 111, 113, 115-116, 123-124, 130, 133, 135-137, 140, 142, 144-147, 150, 155, 164, 168, 176, 181-182, 185, 189, 191, 194, 199, 203-204, 213-214, 226, 241-243, 251-252

Power 7, 11, 19, 22-24, 26, 29, 52-54, 62, 98, 102, 107, 109, 113-114, 116-117, 123, 125, 129, 137, 139, 146, 159, 165-166, 169, 171, 176, 179-180, 182, 187, 214, 225, 230, 252

Purpose 15, 17-18, 22, 24, 30, 33, 36, 53, 55, 59, 62, 68, 75, 93, 95, 99-101, 106, 111, 113, 116, 118, 121, 129, 146, 149, 155, 157-160, 167, 179, 181, 183, 191, 213, 221, 224, 231, 234, 251-252

Recognition 23, 40, 46-47, 62, 67-70, 73-74, 81, 83, 86-88, 93, 96, 138, 140, 143-145, 156-157, 159, 163-164, 167, 177, 184, 194, 199-200, 205, 214-215, 220-221, 224, 252

Reinforcement 60, 73-74, 81, 83-84, 141-142, 144, 194, 196, 214-215, 248, 252-253

Relationships 40-41, 48, 57-58, 77, 152, 168, 186, 250, 253-254

Resilience 32, 36, 45, 47, 54, 97, 108, 124, 202-203, 210, 219, 223, 253

Rewards 10, 26, 29, 38, 45-47, 73, 97, 132, 138, 144, 150, 166, 220, 224, 253

Rituals 13, 23-24, 40, 43, 46, 66, 68, 73, 81, 86, 90, 103, 118, 139, 144, 149-150, 154-155, 159-160, 168, 194, 197-200, 203-205, 213, 216, 227, 230, 244, 253

Schein 95-96, 100, 226, 228, 230, 233, 235, 242-244, 253

Stakeholders 39, 58, 75-76, 98, 217, 253

Strategy 15, 26-27, 30-31, 37, 40-42, 45-46, 56, 58-64, 76, 80, 106, 111, 115-116, 128, 131-132, 134, 137-140, 142-143, 146-147, 150, 165, 167, 169-170, 174, 176, 184, 186, 189-190, 193, 200, 209-210, 213, 229, 231, 233-235, 249, 253

Strength 7, 16, 28, 31-32, 35, 40, 52-56, 61, 77, 79, 88-89, 103, 108-111, 115, 121, 124-125, 127, 129, 179-181, 186, 191-194, 196-198, 201-206, 209-210, 232, 242, 253

Structure 26-27, 104-105, 109, 113-118, 120, 129, 134, 137-139, 142, 146, 150, 154-155, 173-174, 180

Sustainability 25, 39, 63-64, 82, 84, 88, 108, 111, 113, 116, 146, 165, 206, 209-210, 232-234, 252, 254

Talent 25-26, 31, 36-37, 43, 53, 61, 110, 112-113, 115, 133, 157, 175, 184, 189, 197, 199, 209, 214, 235, 251, 254

Team 12, 15, 19-20, 38, 40-41, 43-44, 46-47, 50, 57, 65, 75, 82, 90, 93, 95-96, 115, 124-125, 129, 132-134, 136, 145-148, 152, 161, 163-164, 168-170, 172, 184, 197, 200, 202, 204-205, 233, 243-244, 254

Tools 13, 18-19, 31, 37, 60, 65, 68-70, 72, 74, 76-80, 136, 141, 143, 150, 152, 163, 177, 185, 216, 221, 224, 235, 237, 254

Transformation 9, 13, 24, 31, 37, 64, 117, 119, 132-135, 138-139, 142, 145, 149-150, 170, 172-173, 176, 212, 219, 230, 238, 245, 254

Transparency 46, 139, 187, 200, 212, 220, 223, 248, 254

Trust 24-25, 30-33, 35-38, 40-43, 45-49, 51, 53-54, 61, 63, 71, 75, 92, 94, 100, 106, 110, 114, 121-122, 124, 126, 129, 133, 138-139, 146, 149-150, 153-154, 159-160, 162, 166, 168, 173-174, 179, 186-189, 191, 202-203, 205, 209-210, 218, 220, 224, 236, 239, 247-248, 250-251, 253-254

Values 10, 16, 23, 26, 29, 32, 34-36, 41-45, 47-51, 53-61, 64, 66-69, 71-77, 79, 81, 85-91, 94, 97, 99-100, 102-107, 109-110, 113-116, 118, 121-124, 126-129, 131-132, 136-137, 139-140, 145, 147, 149-150, 152, 156-159, 163, 172-175, 177-178, 180-181, 185-186, 189, 191, 193-197, 200-201, 203, 205-206, 208, 213-214, 216-217, 219, 221, 224-225, 227, 231, 233, 235, 239, 242, 245, 247-248, 252-253

Vision 17, 22, 31, 37, 41, 56-57, 59-60, 81, 90, 101, 132, 135, 150, 177, 179, 192, 195, 213, 255

Zappos 10, 255

ABOUT THE AUTHOR
LEPORA FLOURNOY, PHD

Dr. Lepora Flournoy is a globally recognized executive coach and organizational strategist, and the founder and CEO of Nextgen People. For more than two decades, she has advised Fortune 500 companies, government agencies, and high-growth organizations, becoming a trusted partner to CEOs, CHROs, and senior executives navigating the pressures of transformation.

A pioneer at the intersection of leadership, culture, and AI-driven innovation, Dr. Flournoy is known for bringing a whole-person, results-driven approach to executive development and cultural change. Her client partnerships have spanned industries and sectors, from Delta Air Lines and AT&T to Blue Cross Blue Shield, Randstad, and Deloitte. In every engagement, she helps leaders elevate the conversation, unlock discretionary effort, and build cultures that endure disruption.

Her philosophy integrates psychology, systems thinking, and business acumen. She believes culture is never an accident; it is a strategic choice. This conviction fuels her writing, keynotes, and advisory work on leadership, the future of work, and culture as a competitive advantage. The Making of a Culture distills her decades of practice into a roadmap for leaders who want to design organizations where people thrive, teams excel, and values become reality.

Dr. Flournoy is certified in Executive Coaching, Transformational Change, Strategic HR, and is a Master Six Sigma Black Belt in Process Improvement. Outside of her professional life, Dr. Flournoy is a student of language and culture, an avid cook of international meals, and a traveler who finds joy outdoors and in worship. She treasures time with her daughters, family, and close community.

Through both her work and her life, Dr. Flournoy continues to inspire leaders to build legacies of impact—organizations that are not only high-performing, but deeply human.

For all inquiries, e-mail info@nextgenpeople.com

www.ingramcontent.com/pod-product-compliance
Lightning Source LLC
Chambersburg PA
CBHW020535030426
42337CB00013B/865